Whitman and the Romance of Medicine

Whitman and the Romance of Medicine

Robert Leigh Davis

UNIVERSITY OF CALIFORNIA PRESS

Berkeley   Los Angeles   London

University of California Press
Berkeley and Los Angeles, California

University of California Press, Ltd.
London, England

© 1997 by
The Regents of the University of California

Acknowledgment is made for permission to reprint from the
following:
"Wound-Dressers and House Calls: Medical Representations
in Whitman and Williams," *Walt Whitman Quarterly Review*
6:3 (winter 1989), pp. 133–39; "Whitman's Tympanum: A
Reading of *Drum-Taps*," *American Transcendental Quarterly* 6:3
(September 1992), pp. 163–75; "The Art of the Suture:
Richard Selzer and Medical Narrative," *Literature and Medicine* 12:2 (fall 1993), pp. 178–93; "'America, Brought to Hospital': The Romance of Democracy and Medicine in Whitman's Civil War," *The Wordsworth Circle* 25:1 (winter 1994),
pp. 50–53.

Library of Congress Cataloging-in-Publication Data

Davis, Robert Leigh, 1956–
    Whitman and the romance of medicine / Robert Leigh
Davis.
        p.   cm.
    Includes bibliographical references and index.
    ISBN 0–520–20760–2 (cloth : alk. paper)
    1. Whitman, Walt, 1819–1892—Knowledge—
Medicine.   2. United States—History—Civil War, 1861–
1865—Medical care.   3. Medicine—United States—
History—19th century.   4. Poets, American—19th
century—Biography.   5. Medicine in literature.   I. Title.
PS3242.M43D38   1997
    811'.3—dc21   96-39258
                                                             CIP

Printed in the United States of America
9   8   7   6   5   4   3   2   1

∞ The paper used in this publication is both acid-free
and totally chlorine-free (TCF). It meets the minimum
requirements of American Standard for Information
Sciences—Permanence of Paper for Printed Library
Materials, ANSI Z39.48–1984.

To Laurie

CONTENTS

ACKNOWLEDGMENTS

Let me begin, as this book did, with the late James E. B. Breslin. I first read Whitman seriously in Jim's graduate seminar on American Poetry at Berkeley and hammered out the rough shape of these ideas in a doctoral dissertation under his supervision. He was a superb close reader—demanding, sympathetic, crystal clear—and his presence marks nearly every stage of this project. I owe him more than I can say. I have been blessed as well by a remarkable company of friends who have read and talked with me about these ideas for many years: Mitchell Breitwieser, Elizabeth Brinkman, Kent Dixon, Mimi Still Dixon, Robin Inboden, Terry Otten, Robert Parker, Michael Rogin, Thomas Taylor, and Richard Veler. I also want to thank my students at Wittenberg University, who have sharpened my thinking about Whitman and taught me much about the pleasure and discipline of writing. Ed Folsom, Tenney Nathanson, and Robert Montgomery read the manuscript for the University of California Press and provided valuable insight and practical advice. Monica McCormick was an efficient and energetic editor. Cathy Hamann was an excellent research assistant. My greatest debt, however, is to my family: my mother, Fran Fisher; my children, Emily and Hannah; and, above all, my wife, Laurie. Without her love and generosity this book could not have been written. Finally, I want to thank the editors of the *Walt Whitman Quarterly Review*, the *American Transcendental Quarterly*, *Literature and Medicine*, and *The Wordsworth Circle* for permission to reprint material that had originally appeared in their journals.

Introduction
Whitman and Convalescence

Gratitude pours forth continually, as if the unexpected had just happened—the gratitude of a convalescent—for *convalescence* was unexpected . . . after long privation and powerlessness, the rejoicing of strength that is returning, of a reawakened faith in a tomorrow and the day after tomorrow, of a sudden sense and anticipation of a future.

Friedrich Nietzsche, The Gay Science

"In some cases, the two states come almost simultaneously," Hawthorne writes in *The House of the Seven Gables*, "and mingle the sadness and the rapture in one mysterious emotion."[1] The possibility of intermingled states is the political ideal of Whitman's poetry, and he exploits the resources of the romance as a democratic response to the crisis of the Civil War—the crisis, as Lincoln said, of the House Divided. Whitman's version of the House Divided is not the ancestral mansion but the Civil War hospital. "I go a great deal into the Hospitals," Whitman wrote Ralph Waldo Emerson on January 17, 1863, soon after Whitman's arrival in Washington in the second year of the war:

Washington is full of them—both in town and out around the outskirts. Some of the larger ones are towns in themselves. In small and

large, all forty to fifty thousand inmates are ministered to, as I hear.
Being sent for by a particular soldier, three weeks since, in the
Campbell Hospital, I soon fell to going there and elsewhere to like
places daily. The first shudder has long passed over, and I must say I
find deep things, unreckoned by current print or speech. The Hospital, I do not find it, the repulsive place of sores and fevers, nor the
place of querulousness, nor the bad results of morbid years which
one avoids like bad s[mells]—at least [not] so is it under the circumstances here—other hospitals may be, but not here.

I desire and intend to write a little book out of this phase of
America, her masculine young manhood, its conduct under most
trying of and highest of all exigency, which she, as by lifting a corner
in a curtain, has vouchsafed me to see America, already brought to
Hospital in her fair youth—brought and deposited here in this
great, whited sepulchre of Washington itself—(this union Capital
without the first bit of cohesion—this collect of proofs how low and
swift a good stock can deteriorate—). . . .

But more, a new world here I find as I would show—a world full
of its separate action, play, suggestiveness—surely a medium world,
advanced between our well-known practised one of body and of
mind, and one there may-be somewhere on beyond, we dream of, of
the soul.[2]

Whitman's letter is alive with contradiction. His hospital is both strange
and commonplace, both public and private, both aversive to writing and
the very source of writing. And his America, as it happens, is both male
and female: "her masculine young manhood" crosses gender lines and
exists somewhere between the oppositional categories of his culture.

This is the space of Whitman's romance, the moonlit space of blurred
and intermingled boundaries Hawthorne calls "a neutral territory,
somewhere between the real world and fairy-land, where the Actual and
the Imaginary may meet, and each imbue itself with the nature of the
other."[3] Like Hawthorne's "neutral territory" or Poe's "border-ground,"
the "medium world" of Whitman's hospital oscillates between fixed
states—"between our well-known practised one" and "one there may-be

somewhere on beyond"—and Whitman construes that oscillation as a positive value, the shared, unstable ground of poetry, democracy, and convalescence.

This oscillation emerges often in Whitman's Civil War writings. Like Rappaccini's daughter, the war was both beautiful and deadly to Whitman, both poison and antidote. "[T]he work grows upon me, and fascinates me," he wrote in May 1863, describing his work as a volunteer nurse and "wound-dresser" in the Washington hospitals. "It is the most magnetic as well as terrible sight."[4] At times the war seemed to strengthen the deepest stirrings of his life and imagination, and he found himself strangely "nourishe[d]" amid scenes of suffering and violent death.[5] Whitman's Civil War letters connote a feeling of recovered purpose and poetic vocation. He refers to his hospital work as a "mission," following a long period of inactivity and artistic stagnation.[6] Writing "potboilers" on the history of New York, absorbing conversation and significant glances at Pfaff's beer cellar, Whitman felt that his career as America's poet had stalled in 1860 into a life divided between the tedium of domestic responsibilities in Brooklyn and the ambiguous pleasures of bohemian New York. The Civil War broke up this New York "Slough" and became literally and creatively unsettling.[7]

Yet the cost of this recovery was Whitman's own health. The poet's physical collapse in 1864 foreshadowed a series of strokes that left him disabled and partially paralyzed for the rest of his life, a breakdown he attributed to the "hospital poison" he absorbed during the war.[8] Perhaps equally disabling was Whitman's recognition that the price of what he considered his most important work was the lives of his lovers and friends. The elegies and death hymns of *Drum-Taps* could only be written at the site of the grave, and the relation between love and death present in many of his early lyrics is explicit and inescapable in his Civil War.

Both wounding and restorative, both poison and antidote, the compound doubling of the Civil War emerges in Whitman's depictions of the suffering body itself. "And truly who is not directly interested in these same hospitals?" Whitman wrote in a draft essay. "What family, what man, what woman, in any city or State, has not some relative or friend, or at least some one whom he or she has formerly seen and talked with in health, now wounded or sick, amid these suffering soldiers? Nor is the sight a repelling one only. There is enough to repel, but one soon becomes powerfully attracted also."[9] Simultaneously attractive and repellent, the afflicted body stands between fixed alternatives, gathering exclusive states into a single complex response, Hawthorne's "mysterious emotion." The sufficiency of any single term—"a repelling one only"—is enriched and compromised by the copresence of its opposite.

By 1860 the collapse of a "compromise tradition" in American life had polarized the nation around decisive and absolute questions of morality, sexuality, and racial and political status. Powerfully marked in the sectional division between North and South, this polarization touched many aspects of American public and private life. Driven by fears of racial amalgamation, Lincoln made the separation of white and black the policy of his administration and the prospect of his New Republic. "There is a natural disgust in the minds of nearly all white people to the idea of an indiscriminate amalgamation of the white and black races," Lincoln remarked in a speech in 1857.[10] Driven by fears of sexual contamination, the "male purity" movement of Sylvester Graham, Edward Dixon, and John Todd sought to define and police a normative male sexuality.[11] Driven by the emerging pressure of market capitalism, domestic life was marked by a "separation of spheres" that Carroll Smith-Rosenberg describes as a "Manichean" division between male and female: "Binary opposites, mind and body, men and women, could not be fused," Smith-Rosenberg writes. "The surety of social order and cohesion rested upon their biological opposition."[12]

Binary opposites could not be fused. A house divided will not stand. In politics, economics, race, gender, and literature—the lines were being drawn. "It will become *all* one thing, or *all* the other," Lincoln announced in the House Divided speech of 1858: "A house divided against itself cannot stand. I believe this government cannot endure, permanently half *slave* and half *free*. I do not expect the Union to be *dissolved*—I do not expect the house to *fall*—but I *do* expect it will cease to be divided. It will become *all* one thing, or *all* the other."[13] The powerful appeal of Lincoln's speech reaches beyond the immediate issue of black slavery. Very few Americans were willing to fight a war over slavery in 1858. Instead Lincoln's speech evokes what Robert Penn Warren terms "the longing for the apocalyptic moment" on the eve of the Civil War, the longing for a "total solution" that would "purge in violence the unacknowledged, the even unrecognized, tension" of American culture.[14] Repelled by the crisscross of political loyalties in the 1850s, Lincoln articulates a desire for absolute Union: the end of compromise, the end of ambiguity, and the emergence once and for all of a purged and purified social body. "Let us be diverted by none of those sophistical contrivances wherewith we are so industriously plied and belabored," Lincoln argued in his speech at Cooper Institute, two years later, "contrivances such as groping for some middle ground between the right and the wrong, vain as the search for a man who should be neither a living man nor a dead man."[15]

Whitman's Civil War writings are filled with just this "groping," just this desire to discover and occupy "some middle ground between the right and the wrong." And in an extraordinary reversal of Lincoln's figure, Whitman discovered in the idea of a convalescent democracy—"an America, already brought to hospital," as he wrote to Emerson—precisely the terms of his appeal. That America is not "all one thing, or all the other." Both fact and dream, male and female, attractive and repellent—Whitman's democracy exists on a borderline between pure oppositions, in a "medium world" that crosses and contaminates the deathlike rigidity of separate states.

The problem facing the Republic is conceptual as much as political, Lincoln argued in the House Divided speech. The problem is the agitation of a "public mind" he sought to put at "rest."[16] Posing a powerful alternative to America's "public mind," Whitman's hospital writings dramatize a democracy based not on closure but on liminality, not on a binary structure of separate spheres but on a convalescent structure of crossing and suspense. At once dead and alive—"O living always, always dying!"[17]—the nurse-poet occupies an intermediate ground ruled out by the unconditional terms of Lincoln's Union. Rational and hypotactic, that Union does not admit the "medium world" of the Civil War hospital: its "neutral territory," its "border-ground." It does not admit the legitimacy of a public mind that is both for and against, both repelled and attracted. "In great contests each party claims to act in accordance with the will of God," Lincoln wrote in 1862. "Both may be, and one must be, wrong. God cannot be for and against the same thing at the same time."[18] It is precisely this simultaneous opposition—this ability to be both "for and against the same thing at the same time"—that Whitman emphasizes in his war writings as an alternative concept of Union. "What is any Nation, after all," he asks in his hospital diary, "and what is a human being—but a struggle between conflicting, paradoxical, opposing elements—and they themselves and their most violent contests, important parts of that One Identity, and of its development?"[19]

This is the therapeutic act of Whitman's medicine. "I am he bringing help for the sick," he announced in 1855, claiming the role of the doctor-poet he discovered in Emerson.[20] That help comes as a habit of mind freed from the unconditional logic of the House Divided. As if in direct response to what George Forgie calls the "melodramatic" structure of the national debate—heroes and villains, North and South, good brothers and bad—Whitman proposes a compromised and convalescent imagination suspended between opposed states and identifying that suspense as literally healing—a way out, a way through. "Whether or not Stephen A. Douglas was the man chiefly accountable for the destruction of the center in American politics," Forgie writes in a prescient passage from *Patricide in the House Divided*, "one of the most conspicuous political developments of the 1850s was the diminishing and near-disappearance of the middle ground in the sectional conflict."[21]

Whitman's medical writings respond to that diminishment. They substitute the "separate action, play, suggestiveness"[22] of an unsettled perspective for the reassuring certainty of closure and control. They occupy a "medium world" between separate states and provide an instrument of democratic mediation in the crisis of the Civil War. "We had to have an in-between," the twentieth-century medical writer Oliver Sacks writes, identifying as the place of both writing and medicine the intermediate zone of the convalescent.[23] That need, if anything, is even more prominent in Whitman. As poet and nurse, Whitman places himself in a convalescent space between the living and the dead, and he exploits the copresence of opposites in his writing as a therapeutic alternative to the oppositional politics of his culture and its war. Evoking a romance world between fact and dream, Whitman reclaims a middle ground in the sectional crisis, and offers, against the binary deadlock of secession and civil war, a combination of intermingled states.[24]

That, at least, is the thesis of my study, a thesis I develop through a series of more or less independent essays focusing on the major texts of Whitman's career as a Civil War nurse: *Drum-Taps*, *Democratic Vistas*, *Memoranda During the War*, and Whitman's hospital journalism and correspondence. The range of my study is narrow and specific. I too desire to write "a little book out of this phase of America," or at least out of this phase of Whitman's America. And readers will not find in these essays a comprehensive treatment of the poet's writings from start to finish, from early fiction to the candlelight of old age. Reading Whitman "in pieces," as he said of his own habit of study, I consider only one of the poet's many roles—that of the wound-dresser—and only one of the poet's many Americas—an America brought to hospital. But it is precisely that role and that America, it seems to me, which are most often neglected or misunderstood. Beginning with his writings after 1860, I take as my starting point what most studies of Whitman sweep up into a closing chapter, one that shows how the poet "disembodied" or "depoliticized" his work after the third edition of *Leaves of Grass* and effectively ended his career as a major writer. In many accounts, Whitman's hospital writings are dismissed as irrelevant to a poetic career complete by the Civil

War or read simply as case studies in homosexual sublimation. "After a few short, creative years of speaking to Americans about the essence of democratic experience," David Cavitch claims, "by the outbreak of the Civil War he was virtually worn out as a poet."[25]

I tell a different story here. Indeed I find in Whitman's hospital writings his most persuasive account of democratic experience and I seek to read these texts, as he envisaged them, "from a Democratic point of view."[26] Consequently, my chief concern is to show how Whitman construed the liminality of convalescence as an analogue for a democratic political process. Odd as it may at first appear, Whitman, I argue, likens the ideal democratic polity to an infirm, rather than a healthy, body. He construes as a restorative political value the incompleteness and uncertainty of the suffering body, a body subject to constant change and rendering provisional the conditions of its care. Whitman promotes this incompleteness as an analogue for the desirable instability of the democratic state. Like the makeshift hospitals in which he worked and wrote during the war, democratic government is itself provisional, necessarily subject to the uncertainty of a body politic never wholly comprehended by its own representative figures.[27]

THERAPEUTIC SKEPTICISM
AND THE EPISTEMOLOGY
OF THE ROMANCE

The skeptical oscillations of Whitman's romance have many sources. They record his ambivalence toward a war he both hated and loved. They embrace a liminal play of counterparts he identified with democratic polity and representation. They express a homosexual resistance to cultural categories of embodiment based on sexual purity or control.[28] But Whitman's medical writings also engage the key epistemological debates of mid-nineteenth-century medicine, debates Whitman followed with keen interest as a medical reporter in New York, and later as a wound-dresser in the Washington hospitals. At the center of these debates was the therapeutic status of a drug named "calomel," a purgative compound used to treat everything from heart disease to syphilis, and one that slowly poisoned the patient with toxic blood levels of mercury.

Calomel treatment in the 1850s and 1860s was the remnant of a medical rationalism dominating American medicine since the eighteenth century and setting one of the key historical contexts for Whitman's medical writings. Early nineteenth-century physicians like Benjamin Rush in America and William Cullen and John Brown in Scotland sought the key to medical practice in exclusive therapeutic "systems." Rejecting the concept of specific diseases, such "regular" or "heroic" physicians applied the same treatment to each patient, confident that the same pathology was at work in every case. The Paris clinician François J. V. Broussais, for example, claimed that all disease results from an irritated intestinal tract which overstimulates the body and produces internal lesions and inflammation. To resist this inflammation, the physician must "lower" the body physiologically with a debilitating diet and the local application of leeches. The American physician John Esten Cooke, on the other hand, held that all disease results from a "miasmata" which weakens the heart and causes the accumulation of blood in the vena cava. To resist the congestion of blood, the physician must stimulate the patient through mercurial purgatives like calomel prescribed in massive doses, as much as a pound in one day. Suffering from terrible internal burning, Cooke's patients often died of their cures, or lived on in disfigurement and continual pain.[29]

Despite their differences—they are in fact exact opposites—Cooke's and Broussais's therapeutic systems develop from the same desire to reduce the complexity of disease to a single source—inflammation, congestion—and to treat all patients according to the same rules: lower them with leeches, purge them with calomel. The rules change in different systems but the principle remained the same: an Enlightenment faith in a unifying "law of disease and treatment" that would provide certain knowledge for medicine, just as a unifying law of gravity had provided certain knowledge for the physical sciences.[30]

This faith gives way in the 1820s. Under the increasing pressure of clinical experiences centered in the Paris hospitals of Pierre Louis, American physicians like Jacob Bigelow, Elisha Bartlett, James Jackson, Jr., and Oliver Wendell Holmes urged a "conservative" or "temporizing" approach to medical treatment. Suspicious of the purported certainty of heroic medicine, these physicians put their trust in the healing power of nature, the *vis medicatrix naturae*, and preferred to let diseases run their course rather than intervening with calomel or venesection. This therapeutic perspective was not an alternative medical system but a critique of system, one that emphasized the uncertainty and incompleteness of medical knowledge and sought to build a practice on that basis. "Are you a bleeder or are you a stimulator," doctors typically asked one another.[31] Both options seemed equally inadequate, indeed equally deadly, and many physicians challenged the rigid polarization of regular medicine by occupying what T. G. Thomas called "a vantage ground between the two extremes."[32] Willing to set aside the more spectacular tools of their trade—the metal boxes spring-loaded with lancets for "wet-cupping" the skin, the leather straps for "bastinadoing" the feet,[33] the leeches hidden in the hollowed cup of an apple—conservative physicians were less concerned with definitive cures than with long-term nursing, convalescence, and care. The "excellence" of conservative physicians, Whitman wrote, "is nearly altogether of a negative kind.— They may not cure, but neither do they kill."[34] Remaining between these extremes, such physicians sought, above all, to do the sick no harm, as Florence Nightingale urged, a significant advance over the bloody and dangerous interventions of heroic medicine. John Harley Warner summarizes this change:

> By 1820 most American physicians had become ambivalent about rationalistic systems. Although practitioners were attracted by their comprehensiveness, sanction of traditional authority, and reassuring guidance to therapeutic activity, they tended to regard the therapeutic certainty systems seemed to offer as a seductive illusion belied by the complexity of bedside experience. A growing, often fervently

hostile reaction against systems characterized therapeutic thought during the remainder of the antebellum period.[35]

The professional costs of this change were considerable: the physician's social and moral authority depended on the ability to master and visibly alter the course of disease. But the epistemological basis of that mastery was fast collapsing. In a letter to his father from the Paris Clinic, James Jackson, Jr. voices this concern: "Our poor pathology and yet worse therapeutics; shall we never get to a solid bottom: shall we never have fixed laws? shall we never *know*, or must we be ever doomed to suspect, to presume? Is *perhaps* to be our qualifying word forever and for aye?"[36] Jackson's qualifying word takes shape in American medicine as a "therapeutic skepticism" willing to suspend systematic practice in favor of an uncertain and undoctrinaire appeal to experience.

The therapeutic skepticism of conservative medicine historically paralleled and at times closely resembled the philosophical skepticism of the American romance. The phrasing of Jackson's question—"shall we never get to a solid bottom"—anticipates a famous scene in Thoreau's *Walden* and suggests the proximity of these perspectives, what Thoreau might call the "nextness" of these discourses. "American romance fiction is fundamentally skepticist," Emily Budick argues, describing an epistemology of doubt she discovers, not in Jackson, Bigelow, or Bartlett, but in the fiction writers of the romance tradition—Hawthorne, Melville, O'Connor, Morrison—and in its philosophers—Emerson, Thoreau. "The meaning of the major romance texts seems to have less to do with what they say—about the world, about history, about philosophy and psychology—than with the way they say it. Romance fiction proceeds by questioning whether and what we can know."[37]

Such questioning is not the exclusive concern of romantic isolatoes living in "a world elsewhere," a world "out of space, out of time." Therapeutic skepticism is the key issue in the reorganization of nineteenth-century medical knowledge, and one that paralleled and helped to shape similar changes in American art and philosophy, as many doctors realized. Some "writers are constantly trying to make us believe that medicine is capable of being rendered an *exact* science . . . ," a physician reviewing Louis's work on typhoid fever remarked. "[T]his is a most foolish and dangerous doctrine. As in moral and political philosophy, so in medicine, there are no permanently fixed and unalterable rules which are inevitably true at all times and under all circumstances."[38] The ability to live "with and through what cannot be known"—the hallmark of the romance tradition according to Budick[39]—is the learned skill of conservative nursing and medicine. Open to unforeseen change, the physician abandons fixed perspectives—Jackson's "fixed laws"—and adapts to the complexity of first-hand experience, what John Warner calls "the complexity of bedside experience."[40]

Whitman is deeply attuned to these changes. Placing himself at the bedside of the afflicted soldier, his pages literally "blotch'd here and there with more than one blood-stain,"[41] Whitman seizes on a remarkable conjunction between literature and medicine at this period in American history, one that brought together the therapeutic skepticism of conservative medicine and the philosophical skepticism of the American romance. Naming this conjunction, "the romance of surgery & medicine,"[42] Whitman discovered in the Civil War hospitals the ground of an enabling distrust, a middle ground between polarities by which he sought to loosen and critique closed systems—therapeutic as well as political systems that were literally, massively deadening.

As both poet and nurse, Whitman seeks to tolerate the loss of certain knowledge as a therapeutic rather than a pathological condition. His depictions of sick and injured soldiers emphasize the suspense of a body only partly known, glimpsed, represented, or revealed. And in this suspense he discovers the basis for an unlikely alliance between romantic literature and clinical medicine. An indeterminate future, the absence or deferral of a final word, sustains what D. A. Miller terms the "narratable" premise of writing: "the instances of disequilibrium, suspense, and general insufficiency from which a given narrative appears to arise."[43] But this is a therapeutic premise as well, the condition by which medical care is meaningful and possible. The suspense of the uncertain body is the promise of therapeutic change in medicine, the promise that the present affliction is not complete, not fully descriptive of the identity and future of the patient. The case, as we say, is not yet closed. The dialogue of literature and medicine depends on this "not yet"—the in-betweenness of both writing and convalescence. A medical text that can defer closure and hold open the promise of difference and change empowers that in-betweenness. It makes possible the unforeseen, creatively unrealized future on which both writing and medicine depend.[44]

Therapeutic skepticism transformed Civil War medicine. It freed nurses and physicians from an uncritical (and many claimed, anti-democratic) adherence to the past. It opened medical practice to a larger range of perspectives: nursing, homeopathy, eclectic medicine. And it led to "the calomel revolution" of the Civil War: Surgeon-General William A. Hammond's decision on May 4, 1863, to ban treatments with calomel from army medical practice. But, above all, such skepticism undermined the authority of dogmatic theory, whether of Rush or Cooke or Broussais, and affirmed the primacy of experience as the basis of knowledge. "[A]void an attachment to any particular theory," David Hosack urged his New York medical students in 1814. "Treasure up your knowledge from the sick room."[45] Such knowledge did not depend on traditional practice or inherited authority but on the undoctrinaire individualism Emerson would urge thirty years later: "Leave your theory, as Joseph his coat in the hand of the harlot, and flee."[46]

Whitman praised David Hosack in a "City Photographs" sketch on the Broadway Hospital.[47] As a New York journalist, Whitman enthusiastically reviewed books and articles by conservative doctors, raged against the dogmatism of heroic medicine, and welcomed the turn from drugs and depletions to the healing power of nature as a crucial advance in medical practice.[48] But if the skepticism of conservative medicine is an epistemology of the clinic for David Hosack, it is an epistemology of the closet for Walt Whitman. "[T]he complexity of bedside experience" implies more than the doubts and uncertainties of a medical romance in

Jackson or a family romance in Hawthorne. It implies the complexity of a homosexual romance never wholly known, named, mastered, or made public. Basing knowledge on bedside experiences that included and treasured the homosexual bonding between men, Whitman develops the epistemological implications of the romance in radically new directions.

This is a key issue in Whitman's romance of medicine. One of the assumptions of my study is that Whitman's therapeutic perspective is shaped by a self-conscious homosexual sensibility.[49] Whitman does not romanticize disease as a sign of creativity, as in the Decadent tradition of Poe and Baudelaire. Nor does he pathologize homosexuality as yet another kind of affliction. Rather he shows how homosexuality, like medicine and convalescence, evokes a mode of relation based on continual risk, continual doubt. And he writes the physical body from a point of view that values—and seeks to sustain—that risk as an enabling condition in poetry, medicine, and democracy.

The possibility of a therapeutic perspective based on homosexual paradigms is ignored by traditional medicine. "We looked at Whitman simply as a kind of crank," a house surgeon of the New York Hospital wrote in 1896, responding to John Burroughs's question about Whitman's interest in medicine.[50] "With all his peculiar interest in our soldier boys he does not appeal to me," Amanda Akin Stearns, a ward nurse at Armory Square Hospital, remembers.[51] But it is precisely this possibility that the wound-dresser texts help us see. Rejecting ways of knowing based on mastery or control, Whitman presents the in-betweenness of the homosexual healer as a therapeutic habit of mind, a habit of mind capable of sustaining the uncertainties of medicine, capable of "being in uncertainties," as Keats said of the poet. "[I]t struck me what quality went to form a Man of Achievement, especially in Literature, . . ." Keats wrote his brothers in 1817. "I mean *Negative Capability*, that is, when a man is capable of being in uncertainties, mysteries, doubts, without any irritable reaching after fact and reason."[52]

Uncertainties, mysteries, and doubts abound in Whitman's hospital writings. He explores psychological states based on the intermingling of opposed emotions. He is drawn to medical phenomena, like the phantom limb, which are both real and illusory, both physical and ghost-like. As Michael Moon remarks, he "frequently represents human figures watching recently dead bodies. . . , bodies that have until very recently been alive and are consequently on a border-line between being alive and being dead in the eyes of the observer."[53] But above all Whitman lives and works within erotic relations unbound by the traditional closure of marriage, what he terms the "[f]ast-anchor'd eternal" love of bride and wife.[54]

The love between men, Whitman insists, is different. It is not "anchor'd" in proprietary contracts. It is not fixed in single relations. It has no legal or legitimate status, locus, name, or destination. The names Whitman adopts for his hospital persona—"sojourner," "visitor," "wanderer," "vagabond," "he who goes among the soldiers"—emphasize this errancy, an erotic mobility uncontained by prescriptive boundaries. Circulating through a community of lovers, gay desire defeats patriarchy and sexual possession. It defeats the monogamous "containment" of desire as important to "male purity" writers like Edward Dixon and Sylvester Graham as to the Puritan fathers of *The Scarlet Letter*. And above all it defeats the erotic violence framed by that monogamy, the oedipal rivalry between sons on which, according to George Forgie, Lincoln built his model of Union. That model looks deadly by 1861. Whitman's concept of a nonbinding, nonbinary gay male erotic circulating outside the family romance opens an alternative to the fratricidal terror of the House Divided. It offers nothing less than a new basis of American community:[55]

> I confidently expect a time when there will be seen, running like a half-hid warp through all the myriad audible and visible worldly interests of America, threads of manly friendship, fond and loving, pure and sweet, strong and life-long, carried to degrees hitherto unknown—not only giving tone to the individual character, and making it unprecedentedly emotional, muscular, heroic, and refined, but having the deepest relations to general politics. I say

democracy infers such loving comradeship, as its most inevitable twin or counterpart.[56]

At least that's the way it looks on paper. In practice, the cost of democratic prodigality is the loss of the beloved, indeed the loss of Lincoln himself, and Whitman found that loss a very high price to pay. Whitman's Civil War writings are shot through with a sense of sorrow, and the "half-hid warp" of "manly friendship" is a thread of mourning as well as prodigal joy. "I loved the young man, though I but saw him immediately to lose him," Whitman writes, not once but many times.[57] Perhaps more than anywhere else, we glimpse this tension in Whitman's tentative, often poignant proposals to his own convalescent lovers. "Dearest son," Whitman wrote Elijah Douglass Fox, a Union soldier in the Third Wisconsin brought to Armory Square Hospital in 1863, "it would be more pleasure if we could be together just in quiet, in some plain way of living, with some good employment & reasonable income, where I could have you often with me. . . . Douglass, I will tell you the truth, you are so much closer to me than any of them that there is no comparison—there has never passed so much between them & me as we have."[58] Elijah Douglass Fox turned down this offer, returned to his wife and home in Illinois, and set a pattern of loss repeated often in Whitman's hospital career.

Negative capability is the shared condition of nurse and poet in Whitman, the linking term in his romance of literature and medicine. But it is also a condition of gay love. "Homosexuality takes on a kind of negative capability at times," Christopher Flint writes in an essay on Federico García Lorca.[59] It does not end in predictable patterns—in marriage, in children. It has no foregone conclusions. Whitman's wounded lovers do not settle down with their wound-dresser. They do not find some "quiet," "some plain way of living." But Whitman explores that loss as a medicinal disruption, an optimistic, ultimately therapeutic alternative to fixed, closed, or proprietary habits of mind. He explores, in short, a kind of homosexual science, a gay science relinquishing closure and redefining its in-betweenness not as perversion but as convalescence.

The analogies with Nietzsche are striking. Nietzsche's conception of the "philosophical physician" in *The Gay Science* closely resembles Whitman's conception of the doctor-poet in *Leaves of Grass*, ideas that were in both cases inspired by Emerson.[60] Like Emerson, Nietzsche's physician rejects dogmatic or finalizing modes of thought. He refuses every philosophy "that knows some *finale*, some final state of some sort."[61] And he offers instead a skeptical science imbued with "the *will* henceforth to question,"[62] a provisional science self-conscious of its own incompleteness, and submitting, as Emerson said, "to the inconvenience of suspense." "He in whom the love of truth predominates will keep himself aloof from all moorings, and afloat," Emerson writes in "Intellect." "He will abstain from dogmatism, and recognize all the opposite negations, between which, as walls, his being is swung. He submits to the inconvenience of suspense."[63]

The convalescent body suggested to Nietzsche a way of refiguring this suspense not only as a state of thought—Emerson's "Intellect"—but also as a state of being. And he begins *The Gay Science* with the celebration of convalescence I've quoted as an epigraph, a bodily "interlude" released from the fixed "conclusions of pain."[64] This release from fixed conclusions distinguishes *The Gay Science* from traditional philosophy. And Nietzsche discovers in this release the ironic advantage of his own uncertain health. "I am very conscious of the advantages that my fickle health gives me over all robust squares," Nietzsche writes. "A philosopher who has traversed many kinds of health, and keeps traversing them, has passed through an equal number of philosophies; he simply *cannot* keep from transposing his states every time into the most spiritual form and distance: this art of transfiguration *is* philosophy."[65]

Like the wound-dresser, the convalescent-philosopher journeys or wanders. He remains "aloof from all moorings, and afloat," in Emerson's phrase. He traverses different states of the body just as he traverses different states of the mind. And it is "not health which is desirable,"

Barbara Spackman writes, commenting on this passage, "but the perpetuation of convalescence":

> A stable state of health would represent precisely that which Nietzsche attacks—the immobilization of perspective and consequent scleroticization of values. . . . The convalescent-philosopher moves along the vector between "kinds of health"; like Nietzsche's skater, dancer and tightrope walker, he never touches stable ground, never stops at either pole, never adopts a rigidly fixed perspective. Philosophy occupies this space in-between, the space of convalescence.[66]

In his introduction to *The Gay Science*, Walter Kaufmann is eager to limit this errancy to a habit of thought: Nietzsche "extols [male] friendship and the Greeks," Kaufmann concedes. "But it is to be hoped that the title of this book will not be misconstrued as implying that Nietzsche was homosexual or that the book deals with homosexuality."[67] In an earlier study, Kaufmann had contested claims that male friendship is homoerotic in Nietzsche by arguing that "the overheated and strained heterosexual imagery of *Zarathustra*, especially in its poems, and Nietzsche's later requests for women in the asylum seem proof that his dreams were of women."[68]

"[S]trained heterosexual imagery"—any reader of Whitman's "A Woman Waits for Me" would note—is surely no "proof." And Nietzsche's celebrations of male friendship are not as easily dismissed as Kaufmann might hope, not as easily recuperated as "robust" and "square." On the contrary, Nietzsche exploits associations between convalescence, philosophy, and male friendship as habits of mind and experience that suspend finality—"some final state of some sort"—and he welcomes that suspense as joyous, a gay science.

Whitman stages a similar association. Many of Whitman's hospital and autobiographical writings were written during the poet's own convalescence at Timber Creek, New Jersey, his partial recovery from a series of paralytic strokes he suffered after the Civil War. In "An Interregnum Paragraph" to *Specimen Days* Whitman describes the "half-way" state of this convalescence, a state he would occupy for the rest of his life:

> Domicil'd at the farmhouse of my friends, the Staffords, near by, I lived half the time along this creek and its adjacent fields and lanes. And it is to my life here that I, perhaps, owe partial recovery (a sort of second wind, or semi-renewal of the lease of life) from the prostration of 1874-'75. . . . Doubtless in the course of the following, the fact of invalidism will crop out, (I call myself *a half-Paralytic* these days, and reverently bless the Lord it is no worse).[69]

As a "half-way" state or "medium world" or "middle ground," convalescence provided a dramatic and enabling premise for Whitman's Civil War politics and art. Whitman writes this half-way state into his representations of the body. He translates the convalescent body into a mode of poetry and narrative in the same way Nietzsche "transposes" it into a mode of philosophy and science. Whitman's autobiography is itself "an interregnum"—Nietzsche's "interlude"—a place in-between. Whitman's Civil War writings do not close off or complete that interlude. They do not cure the fragmentations of their subject: the woundings and dislocations of the war. Just as they do not cure their own fragmentations as text: their own inner divisions, their own half-truths. Both poet and text remain partial, in-valid. What Whitman attempts, however, is to revalue that partiality—that "partial recovery"—as desirable, even blessed. And this blessing suggested to Whitman a way of writing the body that could both promote and relieve its strangeness, both restore and undermine its coherence, a writing that could both close and keep from closing.[70]

As an example of this disposition, consider how Whitman both invites and resists his readers' comprehension, their "advance" into a medical scene: "As you advance through the dusk of early candle-light, a nurse will step forth on tip-toe, and silently but imperiously forbid you to make any noise, or perhaps to come near at all. Some soldier's life is flickering there, suspended between recovery and death. Perhaps at this moment the exhausted frame has just fallen into a light sleep that a step might shake. You must retire."[71] Sustaining this "flickering," Whitman both offers and withholds the suffering body, just as he both welcomes and opposes the approach of his readers. He invites us in—"Let us go into [the] ward"—only to shut us out, leaving the promise of the text unfulfilled, or only partly fulfilled.[72] Such writing, as D. H. Lawrence might say, is "tricky-tricksy." But it is a "tricksy" flirtation intimately associated with the feel of living thought for Whitman, with the erotic play of opposed, internally unmastered elements, and with his own experience as a homosexual lover and nurse. The condition of the narrative, like the condition of the soldier, is "suspended." It oscillates between opposed desires—to welcome or to oppose its readers, to say yes or to say no—just as the soldier oscillates between opposed states, "between recovery and death." Such writing refuses to settle down. It refuses to find some "quiet," "some plain way of living." But rather than relieving or regretting that suspense, Whitman prolongs it in his Civil War writings, seeking to sustain—in the flickering of the writing itself, in its drifting in and out—a vitality at risk in both text and hospital.

Ultimately for Whitman this is a political as well as a medical issue, and he construed the suspense of the romance as an analogue for a democratic political process, as I argue in chapter 1. "Where is the real America?" Whitman asks in "The Eighteenth Presidency!"[73] Democracy defers the real in favor of the unforeseen in Whitman's writings. And it demands, then, the same habit of skeptical reserve, the same negative capability Whitman dramatizes in the wound-dresser. The ability to live "with and through what cannot be known" is not only the stock in trade of the American romance,[74] nor only the cherished skill of Whitman's nurses and physicians. It is the basis of democratic representation as well. Working at cross-purposes, democracy obstructs its own tendencies toward closure, toward a fixed or dogmatic political form. The ongoing play of checks and releases by which we write, read, and feel ourselves alive becomes, in Whitman, a democratic characteristic. Democracy is marked not by certainty but by contradiction, not by stability but by "an

infinite number of currents and forces, and contributions, and tempera-
tures, and cross purposes, whose ceaseless play of counterpart upon
counterpart brings constant restoration and vitality."[75]

In the chapters that follow I stress the "ceaseless play" of Whitman's
writings, a vital looseness in the conceptual categories by which he orga-
nizes and represents his war. Throughout this period, Whitman depicts
fugitive or contraband elements that break loose, cross over, and de-
certify closed or unconditional systems of thought. The "ceaseless play
of counterpart upon counterpart" is not an interruption in an otherwise
stable state of health. It is the condition of health for Whitman, the vital
sign of a nation and a body endlessly rocking. As Nietzsche claims,
"Objections, digressions, gay mistrust, the delight in mockery are signs
of health: everything unconditional belongs in pathology."[76]

Gay mistrust is the therapeutic perspective of Whitman's romance of
medicine. It is a gay mistrust in the sense Nietzsche intended it—an
optimistic, ultimately joyous response to the loss of certain knowledge
marking the emergence of a modern world. But it is also a gay mistrust
historically specific to Whitman, one that develops in a hospital of gay
friendships—with Elijah Douglass Fox, Lewis Brown, Thomas Sawyer,
Alonso S. Bush—and one that seeks to imagine an America, indeed
somehow to create an America, open to these lovers and heroes. Gay
mistrust clears a space for that future, that "real America" as yet
unknown. Disclosing the incompleteness of political and medical
knowledge—demonstrating that incompleteness, insisting on it in
nearly everything he wrote about the war—Whitman contests the finality of his own treatment, and promotes, as the shared condition of literature, medicine, democracy, and gay love, the suspense of an inconclusive present. Whitman proposes a way of writing the body that can live
in that suspense, that can greet it, as Nietzsche says, with "gratitude," a
convalescent writing just this side of closure.

ONE

"America, Brought to Hospital"

*Democracy, Homosexuality,
and the Romance of Medicine*

> The expression of American personality through this war,
> is not to be looked for in the great campaigns, & the
> battle-fights. It is to be looked for just as much, (& in some
> respects more,) in the hospitals, among the wounded.
> *Walt Whitman*, Notebooks

"What have we here, if not, towering above all talk and argument, the plentifully-supplied, last-needed proof of democracy, in its personalities?" Whitman writes of the Civil War hospitals. "Let no tongue ever speak in disparagement of the American races, north or south, to one who has been through the war in the great army hospitals."[1]

The "great army hospitals," for many, suggested nothing of the sort. The institutional response to suffering in the Civil War was profoundly conservative, George Fredrickson has shown.[2] Far from confirming democracy, the military hospitals offered a streamlined, hierarchical, and explicitly anti-democratic model of control. Conservative activists like Henry Bellows, George Templeton Strong, Orestes Brownson, and

Charles Eliot Norton welcomed the terrors of the Civil War as an instrument of social discipline.[3] The clarifying violence of the war promised to purge American life of sentimentality, atheism, anti-institutionalism, and freethinking, and so transform America into a centralized nation-state. Distrusting democracy, deeply committed to the efficiency of military rule and subordination, such writers saw the military hospitals as a means not for relieving suffering and comforting the wounded but for regaining and consolidating control of American political life by a dispossessed Northern elite.

Where, then, is this "proof"? What did Whitman discover in his work as a Civil War nurse that strengthened and confirmed his democratic idealism? On what basis could Whitman construe the interrelation of democracy, literature, and medicine, and so identify the hospital as the analogue of his democratic politics, and the writings of this period as the most important of his life?

The answer to these questions turns, I argue, on a series of analogies between text, state, and body in Whitman. Democratic representation depends on a logic of partial or inadequate embodiment. The published text, the elected authority, and the afflicted body are importantly incomplete in Whitman, partial realizations of larger and unrepresented wholes. The visible image fails to symbolize that whole, calling attention to the difference between the full details of the subject and the reductive image that purports to stand for or represent it.[4] Whitman's published texts do not close off or finalize the war. They are not comprehensive, not fully representative. They are instead citations from a larger context that remains unseen: "From the first I kept little note-books for impromptu jottings in pencil to refresh my memory of names and circumstances," Whitman explains at the beginning of *Memoranda During the War,* the hospital autobiography later included in *Specimen Days.* "I have perhaps forty such little note-books left, forming a special history of those years, for myself alone, full of associations never to be possibly said or sung."[5] As an excerpt from his hospital notebooks—notebooks which are themselves abbreviated, mere "jottings"—the *Memoranda* advertises its incompleteness, its inability to realize fully the details of a subject "never to be possibly said or sung."

But this incompleteness is restorative in Whitman's democracy. The problem of exemplification with which Whitman introduces his narrative is an urgently political question in the context of slavery, secession, and civil war—a question not only of how citations represent texts, but also of how bodies represent selves, and of how political power represents a nation.[6] The published text of the democratic state—its visible authorities, its political parties—is also incomplete, an inadequate citation from an America whose full details remain unseen. Whitman dramatizes this idea by insisting that it is the wounded or afflicted soldier who embodies the nation. "To me, the points illustrating the latent Personal Character and eligibilities of These States . . . [are] embodied in the armies," Whitman writes, "and especially the one-third or one-fourth of their number, stricken by wounds or disease."[7] The democratic polity—in a reversal both of his own and of his nation's political rhetoric—is stricken, infirm: not the "full-sized" bodies of the 1855 *Leaves of Grass* but the afflicted bodies of the Civil War.

Body politic analogies are common both in Whitman's writings and in a tradition of organismic legal and political theory.[8] Contesting the social contract theory of Hobbes and Rousseau, such theorists view the State as a living creature or person. Adolph Lasson, for example, in *Principle and Future of International Law* (1871), emphasizes the "personality" of the State as an independent agent. "The State," he writes, "is person in full earnest; it is person just like any adult living man in his sound senses." Similarly Karl Zacharia stresses the completeness or integrity of the State as a unified "constitution."[9] The dominant body politic metaphors in American thought include conceptions of the State as a child or adolescent, comparisons that accent the promise of change and growth.[10] In one way or another, nineteenth-century organismic political theory consistently presents the State as a living, often gendered, subject, sharing key attributes with the human body itself: agency, unity, vitality, reproduction. "The life of an individual is a miniature of the life of a nation," the scientist and Civil War historian John William Draper claims.[11]

Whitman writes within this tradition of organismic theory but he stresses the incompleteness rather than the stability of the body politic, a conception that allowed the poet to revalue the suspense of an unknown or uncomprehended subject. The democratic electorate oscillates between fixed terms, in Whitman's view. It undermines the finality of a settled state with a sense of ongoing suspense. "Disengage yourself from parties," Whitman urges in *Democratic Vistas*. "They have been useful, and to some extent remain so; but the floating, uncommitted electors, farmers, clerks, mechanics . . . watching aloof, inclining victory this side or that side—such are the ones most needed, present and future."[12] Never fully embodied by the texts, histories, or political parties in which it appears, the democratic electorate renders its representation incomplete and so safeguards an uncertain future, an open-ended democratic prospect or vista. Representation fails to close off that vista. It fails to arrest the uncertain "inclinations" of a body politic never wholly known. But this failure, Whitman insists, is a lucky one, the vital basis of democratic representation, and, in this sense, the crucial issue of the war itself.[13]

DEEP THINGS, UNRECKONED

The suspense of an uncomprehended body evokes Whitman's debt to the literary romance. In his hospital writings Whitman exploits discrepancies between public and private, actual and imaginary, visible and invisible. He undermines a surface truth with a sense of hidden depth, the sense, as he wrote to Emerson, of "deep things, unreckoned": "I go a great deal into the Hospitals. . . . The first shudder has long passed over, and I must say I find deep things, unreckoned by current print or speech."[14] Rarely remarked in studies of Whitman, such unreckoned depth is the principal concern of the romance, its "peculiar province," as

Joel Porte writes. The romance is a "duplex structure" of openness and concealment, according to Michael T. Gilmore. It oscillates "between language and impulse, form and suggestion, repression and expression," Michael Davitt Bell claims.[15] Its subject is "the buried life" of the psyche (Joel Porte), "the underside of consciousness" (Richard Chase), the "unseen world of motive and meaning" (Nina Baym).[16] And it is this "unseen world" that distinguishes Whitman's Civil War:

> Of that many-threaded drama, with its sudden and strange surprises, its confounding of prophecies, its moments of despair, the dread of foreign interference, the interminable campaigns, the bloody battles, the mighty and cumbrous and green armies, the drafts and boun-ties—the immense money expenditure, like a heavy pouring constant rain—with, over the whole land, the last three years of the struggle, an unending, universal mourning-wail of women, parents, orphans—the marrow of the tragedy concentrated in those Hospitals—(it seem'd sometimes as if the whole interest of the land, North and South, was one vast central Hospital, and all the rest of the affair but flanges)—those forming the Untold and Unwritten History of the War—infinitely greater (like Life's) than the few scraps and distortions that are ever told or written. Think how much, and of importance, will be—how much, civic and military, has already been—buried in the grave, in eternal darkness![17]

For historians of the American Civil War, this burial raises several questions. The real history of the war may be unwritten, Daniel Aaron claims in *The Unwritten War*, only partly "glimpsed behind the curtain of rhetoric,"[18] but the motives for that repression are racism, transcendental abstraction, typology, and, above all, a romanticism associated both with the feminine and with the South. Preferring a literature that would strip away that curtain, Aaron promotes a verisimilitude he discovers in Grant, Lincoln, and John De Forest, a chastened, tough-minded prose style Edmund Wilson terms the "truly masculine English" of postwar realism.[19]

Aaron's work follows from Wilson's *Patriotic Gore* and anticipates a similar though more explicitly ideological study by Timothy Sweet. In each case, what is at issue is the realism of the writer's depiction of violence. Whitman evades this violence, Sweet claims. He "evade[s] the explicit representation of suffering" in order to justify the bloodshed of the war and salvage a vision of democratic union. The evasion of "the real" for these writers is the sign of a devalued, depoliticized romanticism. "[F]or the ideologically aware individual," Sweet declares, dismissing the possibility this might be Whitman himself, the poet's hospital writings are "extraordinarily problematic."[20]

This description of the romance is exactly reversed in Whitman. Whitman's romance of medicine is the poet's most urgent response to the meaning of democratic representation. The "unseen world of motive and meaning"[21] is the peculiar province not only of the romantic artist but also of the democratic subject, according to Whitman, the province of the body politic oscillating from this side to that side, and the province of Lincoln himself. Whitman rarely refers to the political issues of Lincoln's career. The Emancipation Proclamation, the Acts of Conscription, the Thirteenth Amendment are virtually ignored in Whitman's work, and he chooses instead to emphasize issues of inwardness and hidden depth that affiliate Lincoln with his interests taking shape in the hospitals. Whitman presents Lincoln as a subject simultaneously open and reserved, intimate and unapproachable, available to public acts of portrayal and representation yet undermining that representation with a sense of hidden depth. "Mrs. Lincoln was dress'd in complete black, with a long crape veil," Whitman writes, recalling a moment on a Washington street:

> The equipage is of the plainest kind, only two horses, and they nothing extra. They pass'd me once very close, and I saw the President in the face fully, as they were moving slowly, and his look, though abstracted, happen'd to be directed steadily in my eye. He bow'd and smiled, but far beneath his smile I noticed well the expression I have alluded to. None of the artists or pictures has caught the deep,

though subtle and indirect expression of this man's face. There is something else there.[22]

Whitman sees Lincoln directly in this moment. He looks him "fully" in the face, and seems to evoke in that glance an intimate, transparent society where citizen and president meet in mutual rapport: "He bow'd and smiled." Yet even as he conjures this transparence, Whitman revokes it, occludes it. For somewhere beneath Lincoln's smile, there lurks an unspoken "something else"—that "deep thing, unreckoned"—by which Whitman marks the terrain of his romance.[23] Whitman will not penetrate that reserve. He will not strike through that veil. The "something else" of Lincoln's character undercuts the public, published image. It exposes the inadequacy of that image and provokes a fresh response, a renewed effort to catch the real subject, the real Lincoln.[24]

This, in miniature, is the nature of democratic representation for Whitman. It is the characteristic of democracy to evade formulation and to remain, like the war, "untold," "unwritten": "We have frequently printed the word Democracy," Whitman writes in *Democratic Vistas*:

> Yet I cannot too often repeat that it is a word the real gist of which
> still sleeps, quite unawaken'd, notwithstanding the resonance and
> the many angry tempests out of which its syllables have come, from
> pen or tongue. It is a great word, whose history, I suppose, remains
> unwritten, because that history has yet to be enacted. It is, in some
> sort, younger brother of another great and often-used word, Nature,
> whose history also waits unwritten.[25]

As an "unwritten" word, democracy corresponds with the romance of Whitman's nursing: the "untold" story of his hospitals, the "unwritten" history of his war. A version of what Henry Nash Smith calls "[t]he wordless language" of the romance,[26] democratic representation is marked by absence for Whitman, marked by what it is missing, by what it cannot see or say or name: the unnamed dead of its war, the untold story of its suffering, the unspoken "something else" of its president. The "platform" of *Democratic Vistas*—its political ground, its key premise—is "unoccupied."[27] And in that essay, as throughout his writings after the war, Whitman works to hold open the space of democratic power by promoting a democracy deferred, a democracy as yet "unwritten."[28]

In an important recent book on the body politic in American literature, Karen Sánchez-Eppler describes the effacement of the physical body in political and literary representation:

> An elected representative government presumes that one's ideas, thoughts, needs, and desires can be adequately embodied by someone else. The representative's job is to mark the constituents' presence at the scene of power, negotiation, and debate. Political representation enacts the fiction of a bodiless body politic. Literary representation depends, of course, on a similar though not identical system of proxies: words stand in for an absent physical world.[29]

Whitman's Civil War writings complicate this presumption and enact a very different model of representation, embodiment, and power. Whitman marks an eerie, flickering dialectic at the scene of power: a constituency that is both present and absent, a body politic that is both there and not there. Like its president, the democratic body both invites and eludes political and literary representation, and it demands, then, a mode of thought and writing uniquely open to the unknown. Whitman sustains this flickering—"Some soldier's life is flickering there"—to preserve a sense of democratic incompletion, a crucial sense that representation does not fully reach or realize its subject. This emphasis, however, does not result in a "bodiless body politic"—neither the fleshless personhood of the constitutional subject, nor the disembodied soul of the good gray poet. It results instead in Whitman's concept of a convalescent democracy, an American constituency *inadequately embodied* by its own representative figures. Published texts may stand in for an absent physical world in Whitman, just as public officials may stand in for an absent and unwritten democracy. But the poet does not mistake that proxy for the real thing.

The romance recognizes this tension. It is the mode of writing most alert to the unstable dialectic of presence and absence, the unstable middle ground between known and unknown. "Romance . . . remains (perhaps by definition) unrealized," Evan Carton argues. "[T]he truth that romance represents is present only through and as representation, as promise, as absence."[30] This is the truth Whitman reveals in the Civil War hospitals. Whitman's romance is not the recourse of a disaffected elite, not an anti-democratic withdrawal from the real facts of American life. It is the confirmation of that life, its "proof."[31] Whitman's romance of medicine corresponds with a romance of democracy, and his writings engage the meaning of political representation at its most urgent level: the representation of the physical body. The key issue in that representation is loss. "The sun rises, but shines not," Whitman writes, describing the return of the Union army after the massacre at First Bull Run:

> The men appear, at first sparsely and shame-faced enough, then thicker, in the streets of Washington—appear in Pennsylvania avenue, and on the steps and basement entrances. They come along in disorderly mobs, some in squads, stragglers, companies. Occasionally, a rare regiment, in perfect order, with its officers (some gaps, dead, the true braves,) marching in silence, with lowering faces, stern, weary to sinking, all black and dirty, but every man with his musket, and stepping alive. . . . [T]hose swarms of dirt-cover'd return'd soldiers there (will they never end?) move by; but nothing said, no comments.[32]

Whitman stages the appearance of the regiment in a way that emphasizes a marked absence: "some gaps, dead, the true braves." Whitman's Civil War writings expose these "gaps": the empty places where the "true braves" should be, the unwritten places where the democratic word should be. And in these omissions Whitman implicates the losses of the war within a political theory, one that preserves the memory of the dead within the very texture of the representation itself. The truth that democracy represents, he might say, is present only through and as representation, as promise, as absence.

The empty or unwritten place in Whitman corresponds with what Claude Lefort has argued is the principal characteristic of democracy, what he calls the "empty place" of democratic power. "This model reveals the revolutionary and unprecedented feature of democracy," Lefort writes. "The locus of power is an empty place, it cannot be occupied—it is such that no individual and no group can be consubstantial with it—and it cannot be represented."[33] Democracy is a society without an adequate body, according to Lefort, a society without a "consubstantial" organic totality, without the body of a prince or a king. "Power was embodied in the prince," Lefort points out, "and it therefore gave society a body. And because of this, a latent but effective knowledge of what *one* meant to the *other* existed throughout the social."[34] The presence of the king's body is the ground of an effective social knowledge for Lefort, the "knowledge of what *one* meant to the *other.*" The loss of that body corresponds with a loss of political and social certainty, and Lefort investigates that loss as the moment of democratic emergence.

Whitman anticipates and dramatizes this insight. The locus of greatest urgency in his work is also unrepresented. His political platform is also "unoccupied." But it is not the lost body of the king that concerns Whitman but the lost bodies of the Civil War—the loss of Lincoln, the lost and unnamed dead. Whitman's democracy "remembers" those losses. It preserves, in its own strategic and self-conscious omissions, the unoccupied locus of democratic power, the empty place where the body should be.

This empty place emerges throughout Whitman's hospital writings—in the phantom limb of his lover Lewy Brown, in the vacant beds of the army hospitals, in the gaps of the regimental line. But the significance of these images goes beyond Whitman's desire to mark and memorialize loss. The consequence of democratic representation is to revalue loss as uncertainty, the sign of political suspense. Never wholly present, never consubstantial with any individual or group, never fully embodied, named, or put into words, democracy is continually coming into being, in Whitman's view, continually deferring its own realization with the emergent sense of something else: "There is something else there." And it announces this deferral as the historical characteristic of its nature. "[W]e must recognize that, so long as the democratic adventure continues," Lefort writes, "so long as the terms of the contradiction continue to be displaced, the meaning of what is coming into being remains in suspense. Democracy thus proves to be the historical society *par excellence*, a society which, in its very form, welcomes and preserves indeterminacy."[35] This indeterminacy follows from a society whose inmost nature is never known, never "caught"—a democratic society oscillating from this side to that side and subjecting power, as Lefort puts it, "to the procedures of periodical redistributions."[36]

In the work of nursing, Whitman discovers a way to "welcome and preserve indeterminacy." The nurse seeks to sustain the suspense of the invalid body as the promise of therapeutic change. Medical indeterminacy is the hope of a case not yet closed, not yet finished or pronounced. The ever-present sense of loss in Whitman's Civil War writings leads, at times, to a politics of death, democracy as a politics of mourning.[37] But as a nurse, Whitman sought to tolerate, even to cherish, the loss of certain knowledge as a therapeutic rather than a pathological condition, a staving off of final judgments that recovers a precious indeterminacy, the vital, animate indeterminacy of the living body itself. This is the suspense not of grief but of convalescence. And it is a convalescent democracy Whitman discovers in the Civil War—an "America," as he says, "brought to Hospital."[38]

HOMOSEXUALITY AND DEMOCRACY

Whitman's deferral of the real is not the evasive self-justification many have claimed it to be, not an "unwritten war" willfully ignoring the hard facts of violence and political corruption. The genre of the romance is intimately associated with what democracy means to the poet and with what the experience of hospital nursing actually entails. But the suspense of Whitman's text is not only democratic and convalescent: it is also homosexual. The "wordless language" of the romance, in Smith's phrase, "the unknown element" of democracy, in Lefort's, is homoerotic for Whitman, the wounded body of the lover. Whitman's revaluing of political and medical suspense issues from a sexual relation that has no final or determinate end, no proper name, an erotic that cannot be brought to full closure but must remain—like the democratic body politic itself—oscillating, uncommitted, and aloof.

Whitman's first hospital narratives were published in 1862 in the New York *Leader*.[39] A series of prose essays on the Broadway Hospital, these sketches were signed "Velsor Brush"—the combination of Whitman's mother's and grandmother's maiden names: Louisa Van Velsor and Hannah Brush. Just as the convalescent body occupies a liminal space between categories—between public and private, recovery and death—the poet, in entering the hospital, sheds fixed designations. As Velsor Brush, he recovers sexual possibility: he is "unmarried," as yet "uncommitted." Freed from the patrilineal name—his father's name, "Walter Whitman"—the poet discovers another "reality" in the hospital, a "romance of reality that is ten-fold deeper than anything born of the litterateurs."[40] Not yet named or known, nurse and patient defer final nominations in Whitman's hospital and occupy a deeply erotic, deeply vital in-betweenness.

Heterosexual romances like *The Scarlet Letter* explore the relation between doubt and sexuality.[41] The illegitimate and unnamed child provokes a ripple of doubt in the romancer's world, a linked chain of questions undermining the authority of the father by challenging the basis of his knowledge: his knowledge of his children. Not knowing her father's name, Pearl does not know her own true name. She does not know her place in a Puritan succession of fathers and children and thus represents an indeterminacy at odds with the patriarchal assumptions of Puritan culture. Hawthorne names this indeterminacy, a "labyrinth of doubt,"[42] and he locates the source of that doubt in a sexuality outside of marriage, Hester Prynne's sexual secret.

Whitman has his own sexual secrets in the Civil War hospital. But he aligns his romance with a different sexuality. The entrance to his labyrinth is marked "Calamus," and he explores in the hospitals both a politics and a sexuality existing outside the bounds of marriage. Relinquishing his father's name, Whitman responds to a culture literally tearing itself apart in a fatal quarrel between rival sons.[43] Both sides in the Civil War cited the founding fathers as the ground of their political authority. Both sides identified themselves as the legitimate heirs of Washington and Jefferson. Both sides conducted the war as dutiful sons and pressed their claims in a desperate contest for the fathers' favor. "[W]e are striving to maintain the government and institutions of our fathers," Lincoln declared in 1864, "to enjoy them ourselves, and transmit them to our children and our children's children forever."[44]

But who are the legitimate children? Who represents the father's legacy? Who deserves his favor and name? These are the key questions of the Civil War. But these are also the key questions of the American romance. Who is your father? the Puritans ask Pearl. Perhaps I don't have a father, she answers: "I am mother's child."[45] In his hospital persona, Whitman offers the same response. As Velsor Brush, he is the child of two "unmarried" women, a child somehow without a father, as Pearl imagines herself to be. Whitman never loses his deep affection for the founding fathers of American democracy. He never loses a sense of historical obligation and filial piety for Washington, Jefferson, and Jackson. Indeed three of his brothers were named George Washington Whitman, Thomas Jefferson Whitman, and Andrew Jackson Whitman—living reminders of the patrilineal name. But Whitman also sees how the patriarchal pieties of American culture had created a political structure that was literally killing its children. And he responds to that insight by challenging the moral and sexual basis of patriarchy: its claim to certain

knowledge, its claim to know and name its children. Whitman introduces sexual doubt into the family romance of the Civil War. He releases
the child from the inadequate nominations of the father in the same way
his political theory releases America from the inadequate nominations
of the Gilded Age—"Johnson," "Grant," "Hayes," "Garfield." Whitman's romance suspends those nominations, undermining their authority to represent the real, to name or stand for what is really going on.[46]

But this is not disaffected, depoliticized romanticism. This is exactly
what democracy does in Whitman's view, exactly the suspension democracy depends on and tolerates. Like the hospital sketches, democracy is
written indirectly. It is published under a *pseudonym*—a working, temporary nomination that will soon be changed into something else. At
times this change is grievous, as in the loss of Lincoln, at other times
deeply welcome. But it is nonetheless the very nature of a political
process whose "real gist" is unrepresented, whose "real name" is
unknown. And in this sense, Whitman's democracy is a precise analogue
for homosexuality, a sexual state that could not be represented in the
given names of his culture.[47] The homosexual word, like the democratic word, is unwritten. As Rufus Griswold concludes in his review of
Leaves of Grass, it is that thing which cannot be named: "Peccatum illud
horribile, inter Christianos non nominandum."[48]

In a daring and uncanny insight, the wounded lover of the Civil War
hospitals is made to stand for America, made to embody the "true *ensemble* and extent of The States."[49] The unwritten word of democracy is the
expression of gay love itself. And Whitman discovers in the legal definition of sodomy—what is "not to be named"—terms for his concept of
America.[50] The suspense implicit in Whitman's understanding of democratic representation is confirmed, above all, in the love between comrades, an association the poet insists on in *Democratic Vistas* and in the
1876 Preface:

> [T]he special meaning of the "Calamus" cluster of "Leaves of
> Grass," (and more or less running through the book, and cropping

out in "Drum-Taps,") mainly resides in its political significance. In my opinion, it is by a fervent, accepted development of comradeship, the beautiful and sane affection of man for man, latent in all the young fellows, north and south, east and west—it is by this, I say, and by what goes directly and indirectly along with it, that the United States of the future, (I cannot too often repeat,) are to be most effectually welded together, intercalated, anneal'd into a living union.[51]

Throughout his career Whitman uses body and body politic analogies to imagine the state as "a living union"—not a paper agreement but a human relationship and a mode of knowledge. "What is socially peripheral is often symbolically central," Barbara Babcock writes in a study of cultural liminality.[52] This is the insight of Whitman's romance. Linking democracy with homosexuality, Whitman presents the liminality of the gay romance as a political habit of thought and feeling, the expression of a democratic America he felt more intensely in the Civil War hospitals than in any other place in his life. How then is the State like a body? How does one imagine democracy as a living being rather than an object or artifact? Think of the wounded lovers in the Civil War hospitals, Whitman answers. Think of the myriad scenes of manly friendship. Think of Lewy Brown and Thomas Sawyer and Elijah Douglass Fox. These are the standard questions of political philosophy from Plato to George Bancroft, from Tocqueville to Claude Lefort. But these are not the standard answers. This is organismic theory with a gay difference. This is "gay mistrust."[53]

It is often claimed that Whitman grew increasingly cautious about his own homosexuality during the Civil War and that his "mistrust of the body" led to the repression and retrenchment of his poetry. "If it is true . . . that a great degree of Whitman's originality lies in the radical claims that he makes for the body," Jon Rosenblatt argues, "then his growing mistrust of the body in the 1860s and 1870s may well account for the decline in the quality and adventurousness of his poetry."[54] Whitman's poetry after 1860 "describes a crisis of representation that

Whitman inherited from Emerson," Timothy Sweet claims. This crisis "reveals Whitman's growing mistrust of the body from about 1860 on, a mistrust which was to have profound effects on his poetics."[55]

The uncertain body of the wounded lover is precisely where Whitman's originality lies. It is the ground of his democratic idealism in the Civil War but it is an urgently unstable ground. The "mistrust" critics identify with poetic decline and political withdrawal after 1860 is in fact Whitman's most important response to the representational crisis of the Civil War, a crisis in which the self-evident certainty of antebellum politics—"we hold these truths to be self-evident"—became radically, permanently, untenable.[56] Body and body politic lose their self-evidence in a Civil War hospital. But Whitman transforms that loss into a representational strategy that values the suspense of the body rather than its self-evidence. And the driving force in that transformation is gay love.

Nineteenth-century American culture provided homosexual men with no terms for directly expressing or valuing their sexuality.[57] Shut out from self-evident notions of identity, sexuality, relationship, or the body, homosexual writers recognize the incompleteness of cultural norms. They realize the arbitrariness of cultural constructions that do not match their own experience. And they feel that lack intensely. "The lack of any words . . . ," Whitman writes in *An American Primer*, "is as historical as the existence of words. As for me, I feel a hundred realities, clearly determined in me, that words are not yet formed to represent. . . . [W]hat is not said is just as important as what is said, and holds just as much meaning."[58] One of the realities Whitman feels but cannot name is gay love. The "not yet" of that love—"words are not yet formed to represent" it—precisely matches the "not yet" of Whitman's visionary democracy, another reality the poet feels but cannot see or write or name. Both democracy and homosexuality are deformed by the expressive limits of the present day. Gay love is twisted into an odd assortment of terms borrowed from phrenology, temperance, comradeship, and social reform. What Whitman stresses, however, is that democracy suffers the same fate, the same rough translation into ill-fitting terms or ill-shaped proxies. When Whitman speaks of the public formulations of American democracy, he describes those formulations as cartoonish and crude: "certain limnings," he calls them, "more or less grotesque, more or less fading and watery."[59] The inadequacy of literary and political representation, however, need not dictate what we feel. The lack of words to express gay love does not diminish the reality of that love any more than the grotesque images of Gilded Age politics rule out the reality of a genuine democracy. What matters is the ability to tell the difference. And Whitman tests that ability in scene after scene of his Civil War.

This is the homosexual democracy of Whitman's postwar career. Whitman does not sublimate or spiritualize or otherwise deny the reality of gay love. He does not abandon "the poetry of the body," as M. Jimmie Killingsworth claims. Nor does he "withdraw from sexual topics."[60] The Whitman who emerges from the war to write his most searching accounts of American democracy is very different from our traditional image of a colorless and conventional good gray poet. "In most critical discussions of Whitman's life and work," Betsy Erkkila writes, "it has become almost axiomatic to argue that Whitman's 'homosexual' love crisis of the late 1850s was sublimated in the figure of the 'wound-dresser' during the Civil War and ultimately silenced and suppressed in the 'good gray' politics and poetics of the post-Civil War period."[61]

Most scholarship on Whitman affirms this axiom in one way or another, and it seems clear that the late 1850s was indeed a period of intense sexual and political doubt.[62] In his postwar writings, however, Whitman articulates a democratic theory based on that doubt. Gay representation and democratic representation circle the same absent center in Whitman. Both are written indirectly. Both thrive in a space of creative doubt at odds with the reality of postwar America. What Whitman needed, in short, was a way of distinguishing the unrealized possibilities of American democracy from its crude approximations, its "cartoon-draftings."[63] He needed a way of sustaining democratic hope after the war, and he located the basis for that hope in the hospitals. Whitman discovered the terms for confronting the political crisis of postwar America only by embracing his homosexuality and fashioning from that emotional and creative center a new mode of representation and address. The ability to distinguish the felt reality of homosexuality from its crude public distortions is a strategy of survival for homosexual men and women, a strategy as crucial in our culture as in Whitman's.[64] That strategy, however, is not eccentric to the best tradition of American political thought. Indeed it exemplifies that thought. It is a strategy of political survival as well, a way of distinguishing genuine democracy from the grotesque "limnings" of the Gilded Age.[65]

"I feel a hundred realities, clearly determined in me, that words are not yet formed to represent." Like gay writers everywhere, Whitman feels more than he can say or show. And he expresses that recognition not as a withdrawal from American politics but as an engaged mistrust of its prevailing assumptions, what Cady calls "a critical consciousness skeptical of all imposed categories of identity, relationships and nature."[66]

First-hand observers sensed this quality in Whitman's nursing. Harriet Ward Foote Hawley, a nurse at Armory Square Hospital, remembered Whitman this way: "There comes that odious Walt Whitman to talk evil and unbelief to my boys," she wrote in a letter to her husband on February 19, 1865. "I think I would rather see the evil one himself—at least if he had horns and hoofs—in my wards. I shall get him out as soon as possible."[67]

Hawley's remark conjures a subversive, indeed satanic, hospital presence—not the sweet submission of a "pious bard," nor the Christian spirituality of a "saintly healer."[68] Why fear those gentle souls? Nurse Hawley knew that something else was in play. And her brief portrait of Whitman's "unbelief" evokes the moral and political skepticism Robert Martin and Joseph Cady identify with the emergence of a modern homosexual sensibility.[69] That sensibility proved to be more useful to Whitman than the archaic sexuality of the early *Leaves of Grass*. Whitman's hospital persona does not plunge his seminal muscle into the

American continent or broadcast his seed across golden landscapes. The Shively letters show a mature, passionate, self-consciously gay poet cultivating sexual relationships not with Paumanok and Mannahatta but with Thomas Sawyer and Lewy Brown. What Whitman learned in the homosexual community of the hospitals—the "hospital wisdom" that confirmed his vision of democracy—was how to live a gay life in the midst of misunderstanding and misrepresentation. Such wisdom is indeed modern. Unconvinced by the self-evident truths of American culture, gay writers continue to talk their "evil and unbelief." They continue to share an intense skepticism about American institutions that do not know or represent them.

That skepticism served Whitman well as a hospital wound-dresser and nurse. It sustained and drew strength from the "therapeutic skepticism" transforming American medicine. It found expression in the epistemological skepticism of the American romance. But it also provided a crucial point of convergence in his work as a gay and a democratic writer. Gay mistrust does not threaten or pervert Whitman's democracy. It is the instinct of democracy, "its most inevitable twin or counterpart."[70] A democratic culture recognizes the contingencies of power, Whitman argued in *Democratic Vistas*. It schools its citizens in the "ceaseless play" of continual change, and it thus requires the capacity for "unbelief" Whitman discovered in the gay culture of the Civil War hospitals and promoted as a genuine expression of the American character. We are urged to cultivate that mistrust as we enter the poet's war—to "[t]read the bare board floor lightly here" as we enter his hospitals, to remain "uncommitted" and "aloof" as we enter his political process.[71] For Whitman, as for James Jackson, Jr., there is no "solid bottom."[72] "The way is suspicious, the result uncertain," Whitman warns. "Do you suppose yourself advancing on real ground?"[73]

If the Civil War destabilizes the real ground of American politics, putting in question the self-evident truths of the founding fathers, Whitman's response is to welcome that instability as restorative, as convalescent. It is Whitman's project to defer the real in the convalescence of his hospital—the "real gist" of *Democratic Vistas,* the "real war" of *Specimen Days*—and so make possible the emergence of what is not yet named or known, what "has yet to be enacted." Whitman derives this suspense from his experience as a gay lover and nurse. The body of the wounded lover is not excluded from this conception of America. It is for Whitman the "proof" of that America, its own best emblem. And it is in this sense, I believe, that Whitman identified his work in the Civil War hospitals as the most important of his life, not the marginal accomplishment of a poetic exhausted by 1860, but "the very centre, circumference, umbilicus, of my whole career."[74]

TWO

"On Both Sides of the Line"

The Liminality of Civil War Nursing

The liminality of the gay romance set the terms for Whitman's political theory in *Democratic Vistas*. But it also set the terms for the kind of poetry he wanted to write during the war, a poetry that could cross fixed oppositions and open therapeutic alternatives in the cultural crisis of the Civil War. Throughout his war writings, Whitman associates the crossing of opposites with political and social vitality, the very source, as Sharon Olds explores in her poem "Nurse Whitman," of poetic conception:

> You move between the soldiers' cots
> the way I move among my dead,
> their white bodies laid out in lines.
>
> You bathe the forehead, you bathe the lip, the cock,
> as I touch my father, as if the language
> were a form of life.
>
> You write their letters home, I take the dictation
> of his firm dream lips, this boy
> I love as you love your boys.

They die and you still feel them. Time
becomes unpertinent to love,
to the male bodies in beds.

We bend over them, Walt, taking their breath
soft on our faces, wiping their domed brows,
stroking back the coal-black Union hair.

We lean down, our pointed breasts
heavy as plummets with fresh spermy milk—
we conceive, Walt, with the men we love, thus, now,
we bring to fruit.[1]

Political power grips the body with extraordinary intimacy and force
here. Olds's soldiers wear their politics not on their sleeves but in their
faces, in their "coal-black Union hair." Whitman's nursing loosens that
grip. Under his touch, the male body becomes less monumental, less
rigidly centered and symbolic. The nurses stroke the "domed brows" of
stony heroes who soften and respond, "their breath soft on our faces."
But this touch transforms the poets as well. Sexually ambiguous—their
breasts heavy with "fresh spermy milk"—Olds's nurses disrupt a rigid
geometry, the death-like ranking of "white bodies laid out in lines."
Nurse Whitman breaks those ranks, crosses those lines. The nurse
"move[s] between" the cultural script of "male bodies in beds" and provides a language receptive to that difference, that liminality. The figure
of the male-mother so important to Lincoln's political imagination
brings forth, in this poem, a new union, a new conception.[2] And Olds
locates the source of that vitality in the delicate inflections of illicit love:
"We bend over them, Walt," she says. "We lean down." Bent by that
love, the nurse turns out from the fixed lines of war and death and Olds
cherishes that turn as restorative and fertile.

In the next two chapters, I consider the implications of this *turning*,
this ability to conceive fruitful alternatives to the binary deadlock of the
Civil War. Whitman writes within a culture deeply divided by race, gender, class, and regional loyalty. He writes at a time when America itself

was a nation "laid out in lines." And he imagines his writing as a response to that condition. For Whitman, the ability to reform thought depends on the ability to conceive alternatives to unquestioned cultural codes. He thus uses his poetry to posit links between the members of a binary opposition.[3] This imaginative process relates Whitman's work not only to the "spermy milk" of contemporary poets like Sharon Olds but also to a central impulse in the nursing literature of the Civil War, a literature Whitman knew well.

"My idea is a book of the time, worthy the time . . . ," Whitman wrote James Redpath on October 21, 1863, proposing the hospital narrative later published as *Memoranda During the War*.[4] Whitman's Civil War writings are indeed "of the time," as he knew. His work stands in close relation to nursing narratives like Louisa May Alcott's *Hospital Sketches*, a book published by Redpath earlier that year.[5] Whitman's concept of the democratic artist depends on this premise: not on the artist's transcendence of his culture but on his ability to bring to prominence what already exists in the deeper currents of American popular life.[6] The democratic artist swims in those currents, Whitman believed. He "flood[s] himself with the immediate age as with vast oceanic tides."[7] The flood of popular literature pouring from the Civil War hospitals includes works by Alcott, Katharine Prescott Wormeley, S. Emma E. Edmonds, Adelaide W. Smith, Jane Stuart Woolsey, Fannie Oslin Jackson, and many others.[8]

Nursing, for these writers, undermines fundamental certainties. It renders normally self-evident boundaries fluid and unstable, and it encourages a habit of mind able to "move between" the fixed lines of established order. "[M]ind the crossings, my dear," a military official warns Tribulation Periwinkle, the persona of Louisa May Alcott's *Hospital Sketches* (p. 11). As if heeding this advice, Union nurses crisscross the sexual, racial, and political lines of the Civil War and respond to the cultural dilemma of the House Divided in ways strikingly similar to Whitman's.

NURSE AND SPY

Alcott's version of the House Divided is the Union Hotel Hospital in Georgetown, a ramshackle former tavern she calls the "Hurly-burly House" (p. 18). Alcott began her work as one of Dorothea Dix's "emergency nurses," women called up in 1862 after Surgeon-General William A. Hammond agreed to accept female nurses in Union military hospitals.[9] "[O]ur Florence Nightingale," as Trib Periwinkle calls her (p. 55), Dix sought to transform nursing into an organized profession for women, and her ideas about medicine, disease, hospital design, and administration were drawn from Nightingale's work in the military hospitals in the Crimea.

Nightingale's nursing expressed a medical and social ideal of purity. Rejecting a germ theory of disease, Nightingale understood sickness in terms of contamination and social taboo. Nightingale paid little attention to diagnosis, surgery, pathology, or therapeutics. Disease was a factor of environment, in her view, the result of indifference, impropriety, or filth. Architecture, administration, and moral reform all worked toward the same end: the elimination of disease through the elimination of disorder—any trace of dirt, any whiff of decay, "any hint," Susan M. Reverby adds, "of eroticism."[10] The goal of Nightingale's hospital was perfect containment, what medical historians have termed "a sanitary code embodied in a building."[11]

Nightingale's sanitary code was embodied in more than buildings. Her book, *Notes on Nursing: What It Is, and What It Is Not*, is a detailed moral handbook for women, virtually a micro-politics of the female body. Demanding silent obedience, Nightingale sought, as one of her biographers put it, "to prove that the woman can be sunk in the nurse."[12] To this end, women were given precise instructions about how to dress, walk, wash, and speak. They were told how to read to patients, and how to touch, feed, and clean them. They were told how to move in a sick room, how to stand beside a patient, and how to address him: "Never speak to a sick person suddenly." "[N]ever . . . speak to any patient who is standing or moving." "Never make a patient repeat a message or request." "Never speak to an invalid from behind, nor from the door, nor from any distance from him, nor when he is doing anything."[13]

"These things are not fancy," Nightingale warns.[14] Her sanitary code is enforced by case after case of patients harmed, even killed, by the nurse's carelessness. Devoted to what she calls "Petty Management," Nightingale extends a concept of purity into areas of conduct that seem to have little or nothing to do with health or disease. The nurse is warned to note and control her breathing, laughter, posture, speech. She manages not only the physical environment of the ward but the intimate details of her body: the direction of her gaze, the tone of her voice, the creak of her shoes and stays. "A nurse who rustles . . . ," Nightingale declares, "is the horror of a patient."[15] All of these details are potentially deadly or potentially healing in Nightingale's hospital. All of these details, and many more, are coded by an almost Levitical concept of purity that leaves nothing to chance. "The ordinary oblong sink is an abomination," Nightingale writes, making clear the terms and tradition of her authority.[16]

Nightingale's theory of disease causation was losing credibility by the beginning of the Civil War. But her reforms drew their authority not from medical sources but from cultural and religious ones. Strictly limiting the intermixing of class, gender, and race, Nightingale responds to a widespread fear of social contamination in nineteenth-century Britain and America, a fear that remained particularly acute in Civil War military hospitals where large segments of the American population met and mixed virtually for the first time.[17] As devoted to social and sexual discipline as to medical treatment—indeed these concepts are inseparable in *Notes on Nursing*—Nightingale provided American medicine with a principle of reform exactly suited to the cultural moment of the Civil War. "Despite her well-deserved reputation for tactical skill (if not ruthlessness) in the service of pragmatic reform," the medical historian Charles E. Rosenberg writes, "Nightingale's mind ultimately saw things in morally resonant polarities: filth as opposed to purity, order versus disorder, health in contradistinction to disease. Hospital infection was thus a consequence of disorder in a potentially ordered pattern."[18] Civil War nurses worked and wrote within this ordered pattern by and large. Quoted, imitated, memorized, and dearly loved, Nightingale's slim volume dominated American medicine. "All Our Women Are Florence Nightingales," the *New York Herald* declared in 1864.[19]

A likely story, but only partly true. For even as Civil War nurses accepted the binary logic of Nightingale's nursing, they emphasized fugitive elements that crossed and contaminated that logic, liminal or "contraband" elements that did not fit that ordered pattern and suggested the inadequacy of those conceptual tools. Note those moments, Alcott urges. Mind those crossings. Over four hundred women disguised themselves as male soldiers in the Union army and vivid descriptions of gender crossing emerge in everything from popular biographies of Pauline Cushman to local newspapers like the *Armory Square Hospital Gazette*.[20] These accounts typically turn on moments of unmasking or recognition. Agatha Young, for example, recounts the case of a male impersonator discovered to be a woman by the way she put on her shoes and socks. Mary Livermore recalls watching infantry companies drill in close formation and noticing the unusual walk of a young soldier she then knew to be a woman.[21] Shifting this emphasis, other nurses depict scenes of male rather than female cross-dressing. While describing the elegant military gowns of the Zouaves, for instance, Katharine Prescott Wormeley, in her nursing narrative *The Other Side of War*, depicts a sexual ambiguity she frankly admires: "I have become a convert to them after a long struggle,—their efficiency, their good sense, their gentleness are so marked. Even their dress, which I once hated, seems to take them in some sort out of the usual manners and ways of men. They have none of the dull, obstinate ways of that sex,—they are unexceptionable human beings of no sex, with the virtues of both."[22] Opening the male body to include its opposite, its "other side," Wormeley dramatizes a turn from fixed relations taking place both in her soldiers and in herself—in her own conversion to the Zouaves "after a long struggle."

As "human beings of no sex," Wormeley's Zouaves seem to step out of gender altogether and enter the twilight zone of nineteenth-century sexuality: that of the "unsexed."

One of the most famous stories of gender crossing in the Civil War explores that limbo. S. Emma E. Edmonds (alias Sarah Seelye, alias Franklin Thompson) was a nurse in the Union army and author of an enormously popular nursing narrative titled, among other things, *Nurse and Spy: or Unsexed, the Female Soldier.* "[D]isguising herself in the raiment of a man," as a Michigan newspaper reported it, Edmonds enlisted in the Second Michigan Infantry Regiment.[23] Anticipating the controversy her cross-dressing would inspire, Edmonds introduces her adventures with this rather curious explanation:

> Should any of her readers object to some of her disguises, it may be sufficient to remind them it was from the purest motives and most praiseworthy patriotism, that she laid aside, for a time, her own costume, and assumed that of the opposite sex. . . . [I]t is the privilege of woman to minister to the sick and soothe the sorrowing . . . and whether duty leads her to the couch of luxury, the abode of poverty, the crowded hospital, or the terrible battlefield—it makes but little difference what costume she assumes.[24]

It makes but little difference? Edmonds's tongue-in-cheek disclaimer flies in the face of deeply felt cultural anxieties about the stability of sexual and racial lines in American nursing. Hospital and nursing reforms were prompted in part by a need to maintain specific boundaries between types and classes of people. In *A Thesis on Hospital Hygiene*, for example, Valentine Mott Francis proposed this reform just before the Civil War: "The servants of hospitals should be compelled to dress in clean garments, and not be allowed to wander over the building looking like the off-scouring of the city. . . . I think that, if the nurses and servants should have some particular badge or mark, by which their station and position could be determined at sight, it would do much for the discipline of the charity."[25]

Edmonds exposes the deceptiveness of particular badges and marks of identity—skin, hair, eyes, posture, clothing, appetite, speech. She displays the permeability of sexual and racial boundaries and deepens a cultural anxiety her narrative appears at first to relieve. There are no "separate spheres" in Edmonds's nursing, no lines she cannot cross, no subject positions she cannot occupy, and Edmonds investigates case after case of symbolic, sexual, or categorical transgression.[26] In one scene she covers herself with blood and "play[s] possum" among the dead to escape detection by Confederate guerrillas.[27] In others, she transforms herself into a staff officer, an Irish peddler, an old woman, a rebel prisoner, and finally, in one of the narrative's most dramatic acts of crossing, a black contraband. Commencing "to remodel, transform and metamorphose" for her "debut into rebeldom," as she puts it, Edmonds cuts her hair close, colors her head, face, neck, and arms, and dons a suit of plantation clothing.[28] Mocking the unmasking scenes of nursing narratives like Mary Livermore's *My Story of the War* and Annie Wittenmyer's *Under the Guns*, Edmonds is questioned and cross-questioned by interrogators who cannot discover the truth, the real body beneath the costume. Even her mother, she notes with pride, would not know her.[29]

For Edmonds, the theatricality of nursing demands a fluid, improvisational self capable of assuming and discarding different roles. Adept at Nightingale's "Petty Management," the nurse-spy controls the distinguishing details of her body: the tone of her voice, the cut of her clothes, how she walks in formation. But even as she adopts these roles, Edmonds undercuts their exclusivity, exposing them as *roles* rather than biological conditions, as they are in Nightingale.[30] Edmonds assumes a persona determined not by her race or gender but by the local demands of each hospital encounter, the scene she must play in each hospital sketch. At one point, Edmonds depicts herself not as a person but as the raw material of a person. "I am simply eyes, ears, hands and feet," she says, as if describing a patchwork self that could be assembled and reassembled in different ways.[31]

In such scenes, Edmonds displays the "constructedness" of the body and its meanings. Bodies are literally and terribly taken apart in her hospitals and battlefields, disassembled by artillery, gunshot, amputation, and disease, deconstructed into components: "eyes, ears, hands and feet." Spreading out from the body of the soldier, such disorder undermines self-evident certainties. It casts doubt on things we would never think to question, things we seem to know in our bones: the difference between male and female, the difference between black and white, the difference between human and nonhuman. Edmonds interrogates these differences. She shows that existing ways of experiencing and representing the body, indeed existing ways of having a body, are not final or unalterable. People can be remodeled, transformed, and metamorphosed, the nurse knows. People can be put together in different ways. The raw material may remain the same in each new form—still "eyes, ears, hands and feet." But the meaning of that form and its final, rigid shape are certain only in death. "When he died he was in the act of prayer," Edmonds writes, "and in that position his limbs grew rigid, and so remained."[32]

The radical mobility of the nurse-spy marks a zone of doubt at odds with the rigid pieties of her day, a belief structure based on moral and cultural purity. Edmonds exposes that structure. She exposes and flaunts the gendered division of separate spheres as well as the political division of separate states. It is difficult to untangle those states in *Nurse and Spy*. It is difficult to know for sure not only what is Union and what is Confederate, but also what is masculine and what is feminine, indeed what is true and what is false.[33] Like Whitman, Edmonds introduces sexual uncertainty into the cultural narrative of her war. She explores the relation between knowledge and sexuality so important in the romance tradition in American literature.[34] And she bases her nursing, as Whitman does, on the idea of a sexual secret. "I can trust you, and will tell you a secret," a dying soldier confides. "I am not what I seem, but am a female. I enlisted from the purest motives, and have remained undiscovered and unsuspected. I have neither father, mother nor sister. . . . I wish you to bury me with your own hands, that none may know after my death that

I am other than my appearance indicates."[35] Most everything is not what it seems in *Nurse and Spy*. Most everyone is other than they appear. Whether inspired by "purest motives" or not, *Nurse and Spy* poses a profoundly subversive model of nursing, writing, and identity. Black and white, slave and free, male and female, friend and enemy: these are not stable, viable designations for Edmonds. They are masks, "costumes," the working tools of a nurse-spy capable of assuming many forms. Crossing the sexual, racial, and military lines of the Civil War, Edmonds represents the nurse as "trickster." And her narrative provides a powerful, popular analogue for the liminal politics of Whitman's romance.

A STATE OF TOPSY-TURVYNESS

The writer most present in Edmonds's mind, however, is not Whitman but Louisa May Alcott. Many scenes from Alcott's *Hospital Sketches* are retold with little variation in *Nurse and Spy*. In a chapter titled, "I Visit Washington," for example, Edmonds describes the military costumes of Union officers:

> The military display made in Washington is certainly astonishing, especially to those who are accustomed to see major generals go round in slouched hats and fatigue coats, without even a star to designate their rank. But cocked and plumed hats, scarlet lined riding cloaks, swords and sashes, high boots and Spanish spurs, immense epaulets, glittering stars, and gaily caparisoned horses, are to be seen by the hundreds around Willard's hotel and other places of resort.
>
> I noticed that some in particular wore painfully tight uniforms and very small caps, kept on by some new law of gravitation, as one portion rested on the bump of self esteem and the other on the bridge of the nose.[36]

This is Alcott's version of the scene, published two years before:

> The men did the picturesque, and did it so well that Washington looked like a mammoth masquerade. Spanish hats, scarlet lined

riding cloaks, swords and sashes, high boots and bright spurs, beards and mustaches, which made plain faces comely, and comely faces heroic; these vanities of the flesh transformed our butchers, bakers, and candlestick makers into gallant riders of gaily caparisoned horses, much handsomer than themselves; and dozens of such figures were constantly prancing by, with private prickings of spurs. . . . Some of these gentlemen affected painfully tight uniforms, and little caps, kept on by some new law of gravitation, as they covered only the bridge of the nose.

(p. 56)

Edmonds's passage is a flamboyant act of imitation or mimicry. But it is a mimicry exactly suited to a persona capable of contaminating pure oppositions. Speaking here in Alcott's voice—just as at other times she speaks in the voice of an Irish peasant, or a black contraband, or a genteel nurse—Edmonds demonstrates the instability of voice itself. In contrast to the rigidly prescribed voice of the Nightingale nurse—"Never speak to an invalid from behind, nor from the door, nor from any distance from him"—Edmonds seems to speak from all positions. And she embraces a discursive mobility moving in and out of different persona, none of which can be taken as the real article, the real Edmonds.

It is significant that Edmonds singles out this passage from *Hospital Sketches*, for it is here, in her description of the "mammoth masquerade" of Civil War Washington, that Alcott's revisionary project becomes most apparent. Beneath the gaudy trimmings of riding cloaks and Spanish hats, one finds "butchers, bakers, and candlestick makers"—not real people but book people, not the real body but a nursery rhyme. Even without their riding cloaks, Alcott's soldiers are still costumed, still artificial and made up. Beards and moustaches may transform them from merchants to heroes and back again, but they transform characters who are already transformed, already overlaid with the symbolic materials of a culture one learns as a child.

Whitman builds on this idea. Rather than stripping off the fabrications of culture, he renders those fabrications more palpable and

apparent. He screens the male body behind an elaborate tissue of surfaces—pages, bandages, masks, flags—that heighten a sense of artifice
and representation. He rejects the battle-hardened certainties of postwar realism and chooses, in his most flamboyant moments, to choreo-
graph the war like a Broadway show. "Give me such shows!" he demands
in "Give Me the Splendid Silent Sun," "give me the streets of Manhattan! / Give me Broadway, with the soldiers marching."[37] Adopting the
language of mask and masquerade marking the nursing literature of the
war, Whitman keeps the faces of his soldiers well-hidden, as in this poem
on the Union army's return:

> How solemn, as one by one,
> As the ranks returning, all worn and sweaty—as the men file by
>   where I stand;
> As the faces, the masks appear—as I glance at the faces, studying the
>   masks;
> (As I glance upward out of this page, studying you, dear friend,
>   whoever you are;)
> How solemn the thought of my whispering soul, to each in the
>   ranks, and to you.
>
> *(Sequel, p. 22)*

The regiment files by in closed ranks and seems, at first, to embody the
protocols of male discipline so important to conservative writers like
Henry Bellows and George Templeton Strong. But as the soldiers draw
closer something else appears. The veteran's face is masked in Whitman's
vision: "I glance at the faces, studying the masks." We do not see the soldiers directly but through screens and veils, "masks" and "page[s]." The
real features of the army remain hidden, and thus the real meaning of this
experience is still obscure. Like Hawthorne's minister or Alcott's soldiers, these heroes return if not in drag at least in costume. And Whitman uses that costume to challenge easy assumptions of "return"—the
nation's return to prevailing truths certified by hard experience.

The theatricality of war is the favorite stalking-horse of hard-boiled
realists like John De Forest. "Making no concession to his readers' sen-

sibilities, De Forest took the mask off war," George Fredrickson notes approvingly.[38] Alcott has no interest in unmasking her Washington heroes. Instead she proposes the far more unsettling notion that the face under the mask is still mask, the skin under the costume, still costume. And she raises this issue not only in terms of military heroism but also in terms of race and gender. "We often passed colored people, looking as if they had come out of a picture book, or off the stage," she remarks (p. 17). All of Alcott's characters share this look. Far from being natural or realistic, her characters are stage figures. They look not only as if they had come out of a picture book, but out of a book of "hospital sketches"—which indeed they have. This is a crucial ambition of Alcott's style. Rejecting any claim to know or represent the real body, what she calls "the genuine article" (p. 58), Alcott insists on the artifice of her presentation. She presents the body not as a biological given but as a mask or costume, and she dramatizes the ways in which that costume deforms rather than expresses its wearer.

"An individual cannot be completely incarnated into the flesh of existing sociohistorical categories," Bakhtin writes in a celebrated passage from *The Dialogic Imagination*:

> There is no mere form that would be able to incarnate once and for-
> ever all of his human possibilities and needs, no form in which he
> could exhaust himself down to the last word, like the tragic or epic
> hero; no form that he could fill to the very brim, and yet at the same
> time not splash over the brim. There always remains an unrealized
> surplus of humanness; there always remains a need for the future,
> and a place for this future must be found. All existing clothes are
> always too tight, and thus comical, on a man.[39]

Alcott adopts this comic mode. Presenting the Civil War as a "mammoth masquerade," she loosens fixed roles and symbols. Packing her characters into tiny, cramped spaces, she dramatizes the need for such loosening—the too tight fit of existing clothes, the too tight flesh of existing categories. This is the cultural work of *Hospital Sketches*, the therapeutic work of Alcott's nursing. Like the "painfully tight uniforms" of her Washington heroes, the categories of embodiment available to Alcott fail to fit her subjects. Her characters do not rest easily in their settings, genders, bodies, or roles. They are squeezed into the berths of ships and trains, bunched in families, wadded in hoop skirts, bundled in blankets and bandages. They sleep in coops, speak in whispers, live in houses that look like "tidy jails" (p. 16). Her soldiers are doll-sized, more like toys than human figures. To become a nurse, Trib corks up her feelings and becomes "a boiling tea-kettle" ready to explode (p. 51). Boiling out of the categories that embody and contain them, Alcott's characters spill over prescriptive limits and stage a comic transgression of boundaries that seem, as a consequence, far too small.

"My size felt small to me," Emily Dickinson once wrote, as if longing to slip off the tight costume of gender and cross into a larger life outside.[40] I "wish that I could take off my body" (p. 48), Trib says, expressing her own desire to work in a larger medium, to live and write in a larger size. Wearing rather than being a body, Trib reformulates the physical self. She transforms the body into a mask or garment, and so makes room for an identity greater than its skin, greater than what she calls the "feminine habiliments" (p. 9) in which she must appear and perform. Alcott leaves little doubt about the motive for these transgressions. "I'm a woman's rights woman" (p. 9), Trib declares, as she begins her story. The feminist polemic of the narrative takes shape as Alcott detaches her characters from their skins, exposes the cultural fabrication of the body and its meanings, and stages a therapeutic masquerade in which prescriptive boundaries are exposed and traversed.

What is at stake for Alcott, as for Edmonds and Whitman, is the recognition that existing ways of appearing and being recognized are not final or absolute. Stressing the failed fit between body and self, nurses preserve a freedom of the subject from its historical embodiment. They preserve a freedom of the subject from its publication in bodies and books that are too small, and they thus hold open the possibility of an unwritten, unpublished, as yet "unrealized" "humanness" greater than the terms of its transcription.[41]

As "Velsor Brush" (Whitman) or "Tribulation Periwinkle" (Alcott) or "Franklin Thompson" (Edmonds), the nurse is incompletely subsumed by her public expression, incompletely represented by her public role and name. This is the politics of embodiment in the nursing literature of the Civil War. There is no adequate emblem, these writers show, no body, badge, mark, or role sufficient to represent a subject only partly reckoned or disclosed. It is no accident that these ideas emerge in a hospital. Emphasizing the radical mobility of the afflicted body, the single most profound experience in her career as a Civil War nurse, Alcott depicts characters who move in and out of fixed designations, losing, regaining, and often losing again the determinant signs of a physical self. Alcott does not dissolve binary oppositions in a vague notion of sexual or racial union. Rather she develops a persona able to cross back and forth between oppositions, and she stresses that back and forth mobility—a hospital, a body, a narrative "always astir" (p. 45)—as the possibility of living change. Nurses "rustle" in Alcott's hospital: you can almost hear the slippage. She creates an atmosphere of mobility and symbolic risk—what Whitman calls "ceaseless play"—and she expresses a sexual ambiguity at odds with existing structures of embodiment. "I am more than half-persuaded that I am a man's soul, put by some freak of nature into a woman's body," Alcott explained to Louise Chandler Moulton in 1883, confessing something of her own sexual secret.[42]

In her nursing, Alcott sustains the uncertainty of a "half-persuaded" state. She creates a persona able to move between different roles, to try on and to discard different costumes, never mistaking any one costume for a final role, the final, precise shape of a self. The only garment that really fits is a shroud. "Doctor Franck came in as I sat sewing up the rents in an old shirt," one of Alcott's nurses remarks, "that Tom might go tidily to his grave."[43] What is tidy and silent in Alcott, what is rigid and unchanging in Edmonds, is culturally, if not actually, dead. The comic intermixing of Alcott's nursing confirms what Barbara Babcock calls "the need to reinvest the clean with the filthy, the rational with the animalistic, the ceremonial with the carnivalesque in order to maintain cultural vitality."[44] Introducing a living untidiness into her writing, her nursing, and her war, Alcott turns to just that image. While walking down Pennsylvania Avenue in Washington, Trib feels as if she had "crossed the water and landed somewhere in Carnival time" (p. 18).

This is neither the first nor the most flamboyant crossing in Alcott's narrative, but it does provide a powerful image for the liminal politics of her nursing. Emphasizing the incompleteness of both male and female embodiment, as Bakhtin does in his study of carnival, Alcott describes soldiers and nurses who do not fit themselves, characters whose bodies are somehow haunted, compound, multiple, over- or undersized.[45] She depicts an afflicted soldier, for instance, who treats his wounded arm as other than himself—an "infant" body both separate from and attached to his own. The soldier "was christened 'Baby B.,'" Alcott writes, "because he tended his arm on a little pillow, and called it his infant" (p. 68). "Baby B." is both parent and child in Alcott's image, both infant and adult. Like the maternal body, the injured soldier is doubled, haunted, two bodies in one. Stressing this effect, Alcott depicts figures spilling over the "tight coverings" (p. 33) of their bodies, bandages, clothing, and social roles. She depicts figures who are just on the verge of crossing into something else. She shows the "manliest" of her patients kissing each other tenderly as women (p. 44), the most "motherly" of her nurses preparing for battle (p. 22), the most level-headed of her surgeons operating "upside down" (p. 52). Calling herself "topsy-turvy Trib" (p. 6), Alcott writes the symbolic inversions of the carnival into her own persona. She presents the Civil War hospital not as a site of sexual and social control, as it is in Nightingale, but as a place of disorienting inversion—a world upside down, "an indescribable state of topsy-turvyness" (p. 68).

More than an offhand comic manner, "topsy-turvyness" is a key term in folklore, linguistics, and symbolic anthropology. Marking a reversal or abrogation of existing codes, topsy-turvyness focuses such cultural practices as ancient parody, medieval carnival, ritual clowning, and male and female homosexuality. Symbolic inversion, in one form or another, drives Bakhtin's study of carnival, Bergson's philosophy of laughter, Freud's analysis of jokes, and studies of cultural and sexual liminality by Victor Turner, Rodney Needham, and Natalie Zemon Davis.[46] Despite important differences, these concepts coalesce around a common nucleus. "For Bergson as for Freud," Babcock explains, "the essence of such laughter-producing 'topsyturvydom' is an attack on control, on closed systems, on, that is, 'the irreversibility of the order of phenomena, the perfect individuality of a perfectly self-contained series.'"[47]

The attack on "closed systems" relates nurse-writers as different from one another as Walt Whitman, Emma Edmonds, and Louisa May Alcott. The convalescent, the homosexual, the trickster, and the contraband do not rest easily in existing concepts of embodiment. They do not wear easily what Bakhtin calls the existing "flesh" of "sociohistorical categories." Challenging "the perfect individuality of a perfectly self-contained series," nurses open new possibilities of meaning and role in the Civil War hospitals and safeguard an identity greater than its representation, greater than its gender, its class, its regional loyalty, even its race.

"Topsy," as it happens, is the name of a black slave in Harriet Beecher Stowe's *Uncle Tom's Cabin* and a term often used by Civil War nurses to designate a black contraband in the Union army.[48] "We always had a representative or two of the [black] race at work in our quarters . . . ," Jane Stuart Woolsey writes in *Hospital Days*. "Coming back after a furlough we find the last new Topsy of the establishment seated over against us at the bedroom wood-fire."[49] The "new Topsy of the establishment" in Alcott's narrative is a white, middle-class New England spinster named "topsy-turvy Trib," the cultural and racial opposite of the black slave in Stowe's novel or the black contraband in Woolsey's narrative.

Alcott develops the copresence of these opposites. In her nursing story "My Contraband," a story first published in the *Atlantic Monthly* in 1863, she creates a character who stands somewhere between or above the existing categories of his culture. Half black and half white, Alcott's contraband does not settle easily into one category or another. He is not, as Lincoln says in the House Divided speech, *"all* one thing, or *all* the other," but somehow both—and neither. He "belonged to neither race," Alcott's nurse remarks; "the pride of one and the helplessness of the other, kept him hovering alone in the twilight."[50]

The twilight "hovering" of Alcott's soldier results not only from his racial status as a mixed race contraband but also from his sexual status as a wounded lover, or at least a potential lover, to his nurse, Faith Dane. Half his face is strikingly beautiful, the other half "marred" and "ghastly." Cut by a saber slash down one side of his face, he is sexually as well as racially divided: "Part of his black hair had been shorn away, and one eye was nearly closed; pain so distorted, and the cruel sabre-cut so marred that portion of his face, that, when I saw it, I felt as if a fine medal had been suddenly reversed."[51] Both grotesque and beautiful, both white and black, both slave and free, both self and other (he is somehow "my contraband" as well as his own)—Alcott's soldier is a coin with two sides, two faces, and the Janus-like reversibility of his image evokes the copresence of opposites Whitman emphasizes in his own depictions of the wounded. "Nor is the sight a repelling one only," Whitman remarks. "There is enough to repel, but one soon becomes powerfully attracted also."[52]

Whitman drew from Alcott specific themes in his presentation of nursing. He develops the moonlit resonance of Alcott's night scenes and adopts the persona of her night-walker, her hospital *flâneur*. He extends Alcott's experiments with a medical "ensemble," a collection of rapid cuts or sketches composed along a private angle of vision.[53] And in an act of ventriloquism worthy of Edmonds, he insists on the originality of his hospital narrative in a description drawn largely from Alcott. The book will show "things seen through my eyes, & what my vision brings," Whitman tells Redpath, a phrase that echoes the ending of *Hospital Sketches:* "As no two persons see the same thing with the same eyes, my view of hospital life must be taken through my glass, and held for what it is worth" (p. 73).

Above all, however, Whitman builds the symbolic mobility of nursing into his Civil War narratives and poetry. Exploring key moments of crossing, Whitman defies closed or irreversible cultural systems: the morally resonant polarities of Nightingale's nursing, the Manichean dualism of separate spheres, the melodramatic rivalry of the House Divided. Placing his hospital "at the crossing roads," as he does in "A March in the Ranks Hard-Prest," Whitman intervenes in the oppositional crisis of his culture by seeking to change habits of thought structuring that opposition:

> A march in the ranks hard-prest, and the road unknown;
> A route through a heavy wood, with muffled steps in the darkness;
> Our army foil'd with loss severe, and the sullen remnant retreating;
> Till after midnight glimmer upon us, the lights of a dim-lighted
>   building;
> We come to an open space in the woods, and halt by the dim-lighted
>   building;
> 'Tis a large old church, at the crossing roads—'tis now an
>   impromptu hospital;
> —Entering but for a minute, I see a sight beyond all the pictures and
>   poems ever made
>
> *(Drum-Taps, p. 44)*

The "old church, at the crossing roads" is a place of social and moral intersection. Blurring the boundaries between body and spirit, sacred and profane, Whitman's church-hospital is the site of his democratic faith. It is a neutral territory where contrary states are intermingled or combined. "[W]e are A compound mixture of all sorts," Rodney Worster wrote Whitman, describing the carnival atmosphere of the Civil War. "Stage Drivers Policeman, Hotel & Steam Boat runners Old Sports in hard luck Dry goods Clerks & Broken Down Merchants all mixed together & on the most friendly terms with each other."[54] Relishing this mixture, Whitman recovers constructions of subjectivity taking place "at the crossing roads" of American life.

This recovery, however, is not something "beyond all the pictures and poems ever made." It is not "something considerably beyond mere hospital sketches," as Whitman claimed in his letter to Redpath.[55] Whitman's writing is itself a compound mixture, one that draws on a rich tradition of American medical writing, from the epistemological debates of therapeutic skepticism to the adventure stories of Civil War nursing. Whitman shares with these traditions a politics of becoming. Like the conservative physicians he read and reviewed, Whitman introduces a "qualifying word" into symbolic constructions of power, even his own.[56] Like the nurses he worked with and admired, Whitman challenges rigid cultural systems and injects a ceaseless and symbolic play into his story of the Civil War. Placing himself at the intersections of literature and medicine, gender and sexuality, writing and speech, Whitman "mind[s] the crossings." He too recovers an imperiled middle ground in the Civil War by seeking to remain, as Fannie Oslin Jackson puts it, *On Both Sides of the Line.*[57]

THE STRETCH'D TYMPANUM

Whitman stages this recovery in poems that seem, at first, to have little to do with nursing, medicine, or the liminality of the romance. He begins his war, for example, not in the Washington hospitals but in the New York streets:

> First, O songs, for a prelude,
> Lightly strike on the stretch'd tympanum, pride and joy in my city,
> How she led the rest to arms—how she gave the cue,
> How at once with lithe limbs, unwaiting a moment, she sprang;
> (O superb! O Manhattan, my own, my peerless!
> O strongest you in the hour of danger, in crisis! O truer than steel!)
> How you sprang! how you threw off the costumes of peace with
>   indifferent hand;
> How your soft opera-music changed, and the drum and fife were
>   heard in their stead;

How you led to the war, (that shall serve for our prelude, songs of
   soldiers,)
How Manhattan drum-taps led.

.   .   .   .

   A shock electric—the night sustain'd it;
Till with ominous hum, our hive at day-break, pour'd out its
   myriads.
From the houses then, and the workshops, and through all the
   doorways,
Leapt they tumultuous—and lo! Manhattan arming.

   To the drum-taps prompt,
The young men falling in and arming;
The mechanics arming, (the trowel, the jack-plane, the blacksmith's
   hammer, tost aside with precipitation;)
The lawyer leaving his office, and arming—the judge leaving the
   court;
The driver deserting his wagon in the street, jumping down,
   throwing the reins abruptly down on the horses' backs;
The salesman leaving the store—the boss, book-keeper, porter, all
   leaving.

                                          (*Drum-Taps*, pp. 5–6)

"[T]he stretch'd tympanum" is a curiously doubled and resonating
figure. It is Whitman's most important sign of poetic mediation in
Drum-Taps. The extraordinary liminality of this figure—as Derrida both
explains and enacts in the doubled voice of his essay "Tympan"—resists
exclusive attachments by referring, simultaneously, to both sides of an
opposition.[58] At once private and public, intimate and anonymous, hidden and displayed, a sign of the body (the inner ear) and a sign of the
state (the military drum)—the tympanum resonates between exclusive
categories, simultaneously creating and interconnecting a series of
oppositions.[59] This liminality is visually realized in the architectural
meaning of "tympanum" as that part of a pediment included in the

triangle of three cornices, a recessed panel that connects, and separates, inside and outside within the same figure.

The symbolic mobility of the tympanum denies closure. Both as a poetic figure and as a means of perception, the ear remains an open organ, the one that, as Freud remarks, the child cannot close.[60] The special interests and exclusive loyalties of a divided nation are contrasted in "First O Songs" by the adaptive versatility of both worker and poem. Fixed terms of social class—"the trowel, the jack-plane, the blacksmith's hammer"—are abandoned in the mobilization of the city, just as the fixed range of the tympanum's meaning is abandoned in the mobilization of the poem. Throwing off the signs of social rank—"the blacksmith's hammer, tost aside"—the soldier regains undetermined possibility. The city is literally unsettled by the strikes of the tympanum, which enact the defeat (as the mobilization implies) of social and linguistic fixity.

Single figures in "First O Songs" are multiplied into increasingly complex accounts—squads, regiments, armies, races—in a way that resembles the change in the city itself from an artisan to a market economy. As Sean Wilentz has shown, the face-to-face accountability of antebellum culture, its familial limits, became largely untenable in an urban world dependent on the exchange between strangers.[61] Whitman's images of mobilization draw on this characteristic of urban life. "The salesman leaving the store" perpetuates a social and psychological ingenuity already present in the city itself. The "salesman" re-armed as "soldier" depends on a fluidity of meaning the urban marketplace both represents and helps to fashion: the transposition of cash commodities like "corn," in a market economy, into "shoes," "chairs," "wagons," and "jack-planes."

Whitman's Civil War, at such moments, is surprisingly urban. His hospitals are small towns of suffering and love, and he invests his armies with the restless energy of the cities he knew best, and loved: Washington, New Orleans, New York. "[T]hey are my cities of romance," he told Horace Traubel. "They are the cities of things begun."[62] Like Alcott's Washington, Whitman's New York is a neutral territory of transposition

and crossing. Even as he resists the loss of artisanal traditions in a poem
like "A Song for Occupations," Whitman is deeply interested in the
poetic possibilities of an urban marketplace in which meaning is unsettled. Salesmen, soldiers, and "the stretch'd tympanum" are freed in
Whitman's city to discard and recover different shapes. The transposi-
tions that follow in *Drum-Taps* depend on and enlarge this capacity for
change. The market mobility that changes "corn" into "shoes" in the
stores of Manhattan is part of a larger poetic economy in *Drum-Taps* in
which the body of the salesman-soldier himself—like the commodities
he markets—will be changed into other forms: not only squads and regiments, but soil, rivers, trees, wind, perfume, and breath.

Such poems resist a settled demarcation of bodies and states.
Throughout his war writings, Whitman confronts what Michael Moon
terms the "massive anxiety" in mid-nineteenth-century American culture "about the loss of boundaries between mind and body, of erotic
boundaries between males, of boundaries of gender between men and
women, and of boundaries between races and social classes."[63] Whitman
interrogates those boundaries not only through the topsy-turvy reversals of sexuality and gender, as Moon has shown, but through equally
disorienting experiences of suffering and grief. In "Come Up from the
Fields, Father," for example, Whitman shows how the apparent integrity of the self—its boundedness, its local autonomy—is contradicted by
the repercussions of the wound. The poem begins with a scene of pastoral contentment and prosperity:

> Lo, 'tis autumn;
> Lo, where the trees, deeper green, yellower and redder,
> Cool and sweeten Ohio's villages, with leaves fluttering in the
>   moderate wind;
> Where apples ripe in the orchards hang, and grapes on the trellis'd
>   vines;
> (Smell you the smell of the grapes on the vines?
> Smell you the buckwheat, where the bees were lately buzzing?)
>
> (*Drum-Taps, p. 39*)

The senses are preternaturally sharp in this landscape; colors are unusually bright: a "deeper green, yellower and redder." But Whitman conjures this vision only to revoke it, to disturb it with the drum-like repercussions of writing and war:

Down in the fields all prospers well;
But now from the fields come, father—come at the daughter's call;
And come to the entry, mother—to the front door come, right away.

Fast as she can she hurries—something ominous—her steps
    trembling;
She does not tarry to smooth her white hair, nor adjust her cap.

Open the envelope quickly;
O this is not our son's writing, yet his name is sign'd;
O a strange hand writes for our dear son—O stricken mother's soul!
All swims before her eyes—flashes with black—she catches the main
    words only;
Sentences broken—*gun-shot wound in the breast, cavalry skirmish,*
    taken to hospital,
At present low, but will soon be better.

Ah, now the single figure to me,
Amid all teeming and wealthy Ohio, with all its cities and farms,
Sickly white in the face and dull in the head, very faint,
By the jamb of a door leans.

Grieve not so, dear mother, (the just-grown daughter speaks through
    her sobs;
The little sisters huddle around, speechless and dismay'd;)
See, dearest mother, the letter says Pete will soon be better.

Alas, poor boy, he will never be better, (nor may-be needs to be
    better, that brave and simple soul;)
While they stand at home at the door, he is dead already;
The only son is dead.

But the mother needs to be better;
She, with thin form, presently drest in black;

By day her meals untouch'd— then at night fitfully sleeping, often
    waking,
In the midnight waking, weeping, longing with one deep longing,
O that she might withdraw unnoticed—silent from life, escape and
    withdraw,
To follow, to seek, to be with her dear dead son.

(pp. 39–40)

Whitman discovers in the figure of the grieving mother an instance of liminality as intense and compelling as the androgynous nurse in Edmonds or the mixed-race contraband in Alcott. Self-evident boundaries are dissolved in the experience of grief, and the mother stands at a threshold—"[b]y the jamb of a door"—in the liminal space between waking and sleeping, past and present, her living family and her now dead son. The mother's grief mediates these oppositions. As her tears blur the sentences on the page, they blur as well the physical distinction between her own body and that of her son, both now stricken, and the temporal distinction between the past time of her son's wounding and the moment of her reading here and now. The son's death spills over geographical and historical limits, spreading out from his body to reach his mother. "Maybe nothing ever happens once and is finished," Faulkner writes in *Absalom, Absalom!* "Maybe happen is never once but like ripples maybe on water after the pebble sinks, the ripples moving on, spreading, the pool attached by a narrow umbilical water-cord to the next pool which the first pool feeds, has fed, did feed."[64]

Whitman explores this sense of time in *Drum-Taps:* "a world of repercussions rather than events," as Edgar A. Dryden says of Faulkner's romance, a world where "nothing ever happens once and is finished."[65] "Come Up from the Fields, Father" dramatizes the disfiguring effects of grief. The mother's body responds to her son, remains somehow connected to her son, even though he is absent—indeed doubly absent both in death and in writing.[66] Just as the artilleryman's shell fans out in the dream of "The Veteran's Vision," putting in question the

fixed limits of historical events, the son's death fans out in the experience of the mother's grief, putting in question the fixed limits of the
self. The son does not die in any single instant—neither in the hospital,
nor in the hospital letter. Instead he dies many times, and it is one of
those deaths Whitman represents in the poem, his death to his mother.
Perhaps days or weeks or months after his literal death in the hospital,
he dies again in Ohio. And the false hope of his sisters—"*See, dearest
mother, the letter says Pete will soon be better*"—suggests that he will die
yet again.

This is an idea important to Faulkner as well. Like the child in "Come
Up from the Fields, Father," the mother in *As I Lay Dying* does not die
in any single moment. She does not die when she stops breathing, nor
when she's nailed into Cash's coffin. She goes on dying—as I lay dying—
through the whole course of the novel. Addie's death depends not on
her body, but on her family, on those who remain connected to her after
the literal fact of her death. The "I" in *As I Lay Dying* is multiple, the sum
of these relations, and both Whitman and Faulkner identify the experience of grief as the most powerful evidence of the composite nature of
the self.[67]

The "strange hand" of the hospital letter in "Come Up from the
Fields, Father" signals a crucial opposition in Whitman's poetry. The
letter affiliates writing with death, and forms part of what is by now a
familiar opposition between the living immediacy of speech and the
death-like absence of the written page. Whitman's poetry is often read
in terms of this opposition, and of its subordination of writing to
speech.[68] According to Alan Trachtenberg,

> Whitman wishes the poem to materialize itself in a reader as a voice,
> or to arise out of inert words on a page not as writing but as "living
> and buried speech"; a voiced speech implying the presence . . . of a
> body. What gives his verse its own unmistakable character is precise-
> ly this wish to coerce, to tease, to hector, and to seduce the reader
> into a denial of the experience of reading: a wish to negate the very
> act by which the reader encounters the poem in the first place.[69]

In his reading of "Crossing Brooklyn Ferry," Roger Gilbert makes a similar claim, arguing that Whitman seeks to cross out writing in favor of speech, and so deny the death-like textuality of the printed page:

> [D]eath takes on a purely linguistic guise in "Crossing Brooklyn Ferry," a guise I would identify with writing and its semantic avatar constative language, which act as verbal embodiments of death through the silence and fixity of the page. Theorists like Derrida and Blanchot have taught us to see the deathliness of all writing; conversely speech, particularly in the active mode J. L. Austin calls performative utterance, returns us always to an originating life-force exerting its will in and through language.
>
> Whitman's struggle with death is thus figured in the poem as a struggle with writing, and more importantly with a struggle to cross *out* of writing and into speech, into a form of language associated with life and power, not death and absence.[70]

This argument seems promising for a collection like *Drum-Taps*, a collection deeply invested in what Derrida calls "the discourse of the ear."[71] The resonant immediacy of its songs, chants, drum-beats, and hymns may also seem to cross out the deathliness of writing and return us to "an originating life force." But what we find in fact is that the hymns and songs of *Drum-Taps* are as implicated in death as everything else. Indeed one of the central effects of this collection is precisely that kind of implication, and speech is not immune from the deathliness of the war. In a poem like "Hymn of Dead Soldiers" (*Drum-Taps*, pp. 59–60), for example, not the page, not the silence and fixity of print, but speech itself is the "verbal embodiment of death," its "semantic avatar."[72] Dissolved into "foetor" and "perfume," the bodies of dead soldiers become the breath of the chanting poet—his voice, his spoken words. Far from being crossed out, the dead are indispensable—the very materials of breath, chant, and speech. It is not a "hymn *for* dead soldiers," but a "hymn *of* dead soldiers."

If the opposition between speech and writing is untenable in *Drum-Taps*, on what foundation can the poet ground the therapeutic value of his work? If both speech and writing are equally infected with death, equally invalid as an "originating life-force," what sustains the production of poems? Here again, I believe, Whitman seeks not to designate a hierarchical opposition but to join within the same figure apparently exclusive alternatives. Here again we find not subordination but copresence and coexistence. And here again we find the *tympanum*.

The tools of the trade in Whitman's catalogue of arming in "First O Songs" may remind us that the tympanum is a term not only from anatomy, percussion, and architecture, but also a term from the printing press, and a term that Whitman, a trained printer, certainly knew. As he writes in "A Song for Occupations": "the cylinder press . . the handpress . . the frisket and tympan."[73] The tympan, in a printing press, is a frame covered with a sheet of silk or parchment on which a leaf of paper is positioned and held by the frisket. On a handpress, the tympan is itself doubled into interlocking frames nested or lodged within one another.[74] The overlapping of discursive realms in Whitman's use of the word (architecture, anatomy, percussion, printing) is reproduced in the design of the press itself. The printer's tympan suggests not only the shape of the ear but the composite layering so important to Whitman's collection as a whole.

The very term that appears to inscribe the opposition between speech and writing is in fact copresent to both sides. A term of uncanny mediation, the tympanum is not merely present in the discourse of speech and writing but formally and technically indispensable to those discourses, the very means of their production. In his hospital narratives Whitman will act out the meaning of this mediation, testing the limits of his sympathy to stretch across the political and social oppositions of the war. In *Drum-Taps* Whitman discovers and implicates that mediation in the very production of the poem. The tympanum does not cross out the companion terms of Whitman's art—the deathliness of writing, the silence of the printed page—just as the poet does not cross out or subordinate the companion terms of the Civil War—the Confederacy, the "secesh." Instead the tympanum is a source of poetic and political equalization for Whitman, one that makes possible a simultaneous opposition, a composite identity, a federated union.

For Whitman, the end of the Civil War inaugurated an era of social and political consolidation in American life that misunderstood and dishonored the complex figure of its own war. For the rest of his life Whitman would try to keep that war alive as a counteractant to the aggressive and morally indifferent materialism of postwar culture. The liminal figures in his work look increasingly naive to a postwar generation in which male and female, rational and imaginative, urban and rural, public and private, expert and amateur harden into pure oppositions—each term, in Donne's phrase, "intire of it selfe."

In each of its characteristics—its battles, its deaths, its grieving mothers—the figures of war are mixed, crossed, intricately layered. Even the dead, we find in "Dirge for Two Veterans," are stacked in a "double grave" (*Sequel*, p. 21). The irony of the Civil War is the fact that "enemies" are at the same time "brothers," "sisters," "fathers," "friends," and "lovers." Like the nurse, the contraband, and the homosexual—the soldier is more than himself, more than he first appears. Civil War nurses exploit this irony by staging moments of symbolic and sexual reversal that open the body to include its opposite—its other "face" in Alcott, its "other side" in Wormeley. Whitman exploits this irony by showing how a set of opposed terms within poetry itself—the opposition between speech and writing—turn out in fact to overlap one another in the complex figure of the tympanum. This overlapping is the formal condition of the *Sequel to Drum-Taps*, and its central poetic subject, a subject enacted both in the overlapping of voices in "When Lilacs Last in the Dooryard Bloom'd" and in the overlapping of bodies in "As I Lay with My Head in Your Lap Camerado." The intimate enfolding of lovers, the overlapping of discursive realms, the liminality of complex figures, the intermingling of opposed states: these are the terms of literary and cultural vitality in Whitman's work, and the weapons with which he fought the Civil War.

THREE

Sympathy and the Crisis of Union

Compassion is a very untenable ground. It must be
expeditious. Its pleadings will not bear to be stereotyped.
Henry David Thoreau, Walden

In one of his last depictions of Civil War nursing, Whitman recalls this
scene from the Douglas Hospital:

> In one of [the wards] found an old acquaintance transferr'd here
> lately, a rebel prisoner, in a dying condition. Poor fellow, the look
> was already on his face. He gazed long at me. I ask'd him if he knew
> me. After a moment he utter'd something, but inarticulately. I have
> seen him off and on for the last five months. He has suffer'd very
> much; a bad wound in left leg, severely fractured, several operations,
> cuttings, extractions of bone, splinters, &c. I remember he seem'd to
> me, as I used to talk with him, a fair specimen of the main strata of
> the Southerners, those without property or education, but still with
> the stamp which comes from freedom and equality. . . . He made no
> outward show, was mild in his talk and behavior, but I knew he wor-

ried much inwardly. But now all would be over very soon. I half sat
upon the little stand near the head of the bed. Wallace was somewhat restless. I placed my hand lightly on his forehead and face, just
sliding it over the surface. In a moment or so he fell into a calm,
regular-breathing lethargy or sleep, and remain'd so while I sat
there.[1]

The scene is both personal and political. It evokes the tenderness Whitman felt for the wounded and exemplifies the kind of writing he valued
most in accounts of the war. But the passage also alludes to class conflicts
central to Whitman's interpretation of the Civil War. For Whitman the
key issue in the Civil War was the future of white workingmen on both
sides of the line.[2] The war was caused, he believed, not by slavery, but by
a "despotism" of special interests manipulating political events in the
1850s and victimizing "the great masses of the people."[3] The rebel soldier is one of those victims, part of that great mass. We don't know of
course whether Jonathan Wallace shared this view, indeed whether he
believed in the Free Soil ideology his suffering now supports. "[H]e
utter'd something," Whitman says, "but inarticulately." Lacking both
property and voice, the soldier dies into an idea. He becomes a type or
example, another "fair specimen." Just sliding over the surface of social
discord, Whitman, at such moments, neutralizes disaffection and
soothes an inner restlessness worrying both nation and poet.[4]

   "Standing his lonely vigil upon the battlefields of death or marching
through the darkness of Virginia," James Cox writes, "the poet expresses
even across the gulf of Civil War the old urge toward union, adhesive-
ness, coherence, love, striving to preserve the Union in his name."[5] This
is a view Whitman believed in and sought to promote. The image of the
poet standing his lonely vigil of Union recalls the wound-dresser pane-
gyrics William O'Connor, Richard Maurice Bucke, and Thomas Don-
aldson began writing after the war. The poet's official desire to regather
the "debris and debris"[6] of a nation and a poetic violated by death and
reaffirm "the old urge toward union" is well documented in his major

texts and in their criticism. What is less well understood is the way in which Whitman's writings rebel against this dominant impulse and display the signs of incompleteness, incongruence, and paradox—the signs of "an inner civil war."

Whitman's concept of sympathy is a local version of this issue. Like so much in his war, Whitman's sympathy has two sides, two faces. Drawing on a tradition in the sentimental novel, Whitman deploys a normalizing rhetoric of compassion in his war writings, one that overcomes the estrangement of the other with an intimate discourse of social belonging and love. In the midst of that normalization, however, Whitman calls attention to the ways in which the objects of compassion exceed their recuperative containment and make possible politically and psychologically necessary forms of divergence. Brought in from the outside, literally in from the "Wilderness" of Northern Virginia, Whitman's soldiers are restored to normative modes of discourse and social relation. But they do not remain fully settled within the terms of that relation, retaining instead a fugitive strangeness unremediated by the proffered assurance of closure, regularity, homogeneity, or Union. Importantly doubled, Whitman's sympathy both repairs the coherence of a world riddled by death and safeguards what he calls "the precious idiocrasy" of an individual self, a self whose inwardness cannot be fully shared or appropriated by others.[7] This counter-impulse expresses a desire not to soothe but to stir attention, to assault the "lethargy" of a complacent mind, and to guard against forms of Union that would regularize the eccentric rhythms of his experience. Leaving key elements of his war cryptic, conflicted, and significantly textual, Whitman refounds the distinction between public and private and articulates a sympathetic relation in which self and other remain simultaneously, paradoxically, intimate and strange.

THE OUTCAST WANDERER

The effect of sympathy as a disruptive or defamiliarizing force crosses the grain of Whitman's tendency to construe his work as the recuperation of the stranger. This habit of mind is deeply affiliated with Whitman's understanding of sympathy, and indeed with the 1855 *Leaves of Grass* itself, a book modeled in its design and mode of address on the sentimental novelist Fanny Fern (Sara Parton). Sentimental writers like Fanny Fern and Harriet Beecher Stowe had a more profound effect on Whitman than is usually recognized, a fact owing to the poet's determined effort to distinguish himself from a tradition of literary sentimentality. But Stowe's phenomenal success as a novelist provided tangible evidence for the kind of mass readership Whitman imagined for his own work.[8] "The proof of a poet is that his country absorbs him as affectionately as he has absorbed it," Whitman claimed in the 1855 Preface.[9] Whitman's boast seems slightly less naive given the success of *Uncle Tom's Cabin*, a book that America had indeed "absorbed" in 1852. After five years of neglect and public indifference, Whitman brought out the third edition of *Leaves of Grass* with Stowe's accomplishment still very much on his mind: "expect [*Leaves of Grass*] to be a valuable investment," Whitman wrote his brother in 1860, "increasing by months and years—not going off in a rocket way, (like 'Uncle Tom's Cabin')."[10]

The Civil War closed the gap between these writers, and Whitman turned to *Uncle Tom's Cabin* not as a way of contrasting his own literary prospects, but as a demonstration of how literature could become a moral force in American life. The crisis of national union for Whitman, like the crisis of slavery for Stowe, is localized in the intimacy of a subjective encounter. Compassion for the suffering of others is the felt demonstration of union for Stowe and Whitman, the experiential ground from which political ideals are drawn. Public policy is a displaced and expanded form of private feeling, sentimentality asserts, the extension of intimate forms of relation into wider political realms. American political rhetoric before the Civil War—preeminently in the writings and speeches of Edward Everett—responded to what many perceived as the increasing distance between private feeling and public role. And it is this separation of public from private, politics from love, that sentimentality identifies as the source of a national crisis.[11]

The cultural work of *Uncle Tom's Cabin* was to reproduce for a white audience an emotional equivalent for slavery and so respond to the dilemma of national disunion by healing the inner division between head and heart. The public institution of slavery is reformulated by Stowe in the intimacy of a sympathetic encounter, just as the settings of the novel—Rachel's kitchen, Little Eva's bedside, Legree's attic—bring the slave into private space. According to Jane Tompkins, "sentimental novels take place, metaphorically and literally, in the 'closet.' Sentimental heroines rarely get beyond the confines of a private space—the kitchen, the parlor, the upstairs chamber—but more important, most of what they do takes place inside the 'closet' of the heart. For what the word *sentimental* really means in this context is that the arena of human action . . . has been defined not as the world, but as the human soul."[12]

This is clearly Whitman's intention in reducing the massive scale of the Civil War to the narrower limits of the Washington hospital, and in reconceiving the epistemological and political issues of disunion in terms of a subjective encounter with the suffering soldier. The direction of poetic development is inward in Whitman—from the battlefield to the bivouac reverie, from the gunshot wound in the child's breast to the stricken soul of his mother, from the physical suffering of the patient to the emotional suffering of the nurse. "[T]he marrow of the tragedy [was] concentrated in those Hospitals," Whitman writes; "(it seem'd sometimes as if the whole interest of the land, North and South, was one vast central hospital, and all the rest of the affair but flanges)."[13] However central nursing and medicine were to the Civil War, they did not monopolize "the whole interest of the land, North and South." Whitman's image of a vast hospital stretching across the American continent evokes the conflict between his need to reduce and internalize the arena of meaningful action and his recognition of the coercion that reduction entails.

Whitman seeks at times to distance himself from the literary and political conventions of sentimentality, and he found in the cool efficiency of the military surgeon a compelling alternative to the tradition of gentle feeling. Commenting on a surgeon's pragmatic response to death, Whitman writes approvingly: "There is no fuss made. Not a bit of sentimentalism or whining have I seen about a single death-bed in hospital or on the field, but generally impassive indifference" (p. 736). "[I]mpassive indifference" often horrified Nurse Whitman, and his off-hand rejection of "sentimentalism" must be qualified by the sense of his deep affiliation with its central themes. In particular, sentimentality provided Whitman with a powerful way of reconnecting his emotional experience as a hospital nurse with much broader national issues and of thus strengthening the poet's belief in the public value of his private life, a belief on which Whitman's success as a writer largely depended.[14] Whitman's Washington notebooks are marked by a strong sense of the poet's alienation from conventional politics. "Look at the little mammi-kins," Whitman wrote after watching a series of congressional debates in 1863, "shrewd, gabby, drest in black, hopping about, making motions, amendments."[15] Repelled by the shallowness of the War Congress, a Congress that seemed to him unfeeling, almost mechanical, Whitman recovered in his nursing the emotional sources of his politics and art.

In *Uncle Tom's Cabin*, Stowe encourages her reader to substitute the intimacy of Little Eva's death for the strangeness of the experience of slavery. Rewriting "slavery" as "the loss of a child," as Philip Fisher has shown, Stowe makes possible a sympathetic identification between reader and slave. Fisher writes:

> The sentimental novel creates the extension of feeling on which the restitution of humanity is based by means of equations between the deep common feelings of the reader and the exotic but analogous situations of the characters. The 19th-century reader of Stowe's novel had no experience of having a member of his family suddenly sold off to a distant plantation from which he would never return, but the reader did almost certainly undergo traumatic, unexpected separation from someone, often a child, by death. The unexpected death of the only child, the center of the family's life, is, therefore, the experiential equation, dramatized in the death of Little Eva, by

means of which the reader can cross over to the inner world of the slave family.[16]

The death of a beloved child is what slavery feels like, Stowe shows. It is the experiential analogue for what is otherwise wholly outside the subjectivity of her white audience. As long as her reader is willing to equate the death of the child with analogous forms of loss, grief forms the basis for a reunifying experience of sympathy.

Whitman develops this idea by identifying the hospital as the marrow and metonym of the Civil War. It is not the alien experience of slavery that drives this change, however, but Whitman's own alienation from American political life, from the "little mannikins" of the Thirty-seventh Congress. The Civil War hospital restored an intimacy and emotional depth to Whitman's conception of Union by enabling him to exchange for such figures the undeniable tenderness he felt for the wounded and thus to reconceive as marginal, mere "flanges," subjects for whom he could generate little interest. "As this tremendous war goes on, the public interest becomes more general and gathers more and more closely about the wounded, the sick, the great Government Hospitals," Whitman wrote in a New York *Times* article in 1864. "Every family has directly or indirectly some representative among this vast army of the wounded and sick."[17]

Just as Stowe substitutes the death of Little Eva for the alien experience of the black slave, Whitman substitutes the death of the child-soldier for the alien experience of the political mannikin. In the politics of Whitman's sympathy, the child becomes the nation's "representative" in a Congress of the wounded, and the shared experience of loss becomes the subjective ground of national reunion. The substitutional logic of such sympathy allowed Whitman to affiliate the meaning of the war with his own experience in the hospitals, and so recover the empowering but intermittent sense that his private feelings held the key to the nation's hope.

"[W]e must put aside our private feelings," Senator Bird tells his wife, Mary, in his justification of the Fugitive Slave Law in *Uncle Tom's Cabin*, when "there are great public interests involved."[18] Bird's defense of slavery depends on the division between public and private Stowe's novel and Whitman's poetry seek to repair. As Stowe's chapter unfolds, the Fugitive Slave Law becomes meaningful to John Bird, this policy becomes personal, when the escaped slave Eliza arrives at the Birds' home seeking help for herself and her son Harry. Searching for a basis of shared feeling, Eliza asks Mary Bird, "Ma'am . . . have you ever lost a child? . . . Then you will feel for me."[19] Senator Bird's binary rhetoric is transformed and deepened by Eliza's question, as it turns him toward the memory of the loss of his own son Henry. As Eliza's question reopens that memory, John and Mary enter and reopen Henry's bedroom and bureau, and offer Eliza's child the intimate tokens of a now public grief:

> Mrs. Bird slowly opened the drawer. There were little coats of many a form and pattern, piles of aprons, and rows of small stockings; and even a pair of little shoes, worn and rubbed at the toes, were peeping from the folds of a paper. There was a toy horse and wagon, a top, a ball,—memorials gathered with many a tear and many a heart-break! She sat down by the drawer, and, leaning her head on her hands over it, wept till the tears fell through her fingers into the drawer; then suddenly raising her head, she began, with nervous haste, selecting the plainest and most substantial articles, and gathering them into a bundle.[20]

The effect of the Birds' sympathy is to bring the stranger in from the outside, in from the wilderness, and to resignify social belonging with the intimate tokens of affection. As the slave child is re-dressed in the son's clothing, the Birds' sympathy allows the slave figuratively to become "Henry," reminding the Senator not of public policy but of private grief. Like the soft fabric of Stowe's prose, Henry's clothing recontains the fugitive threat of the slave within the familiarity of well-known signs, the shoes scuffed and worn. But like the clothing, the Birds' sympathy is importantly *second-hand*, conceived in the relation with their son and now loaned out to a larger world. And in this way their sympathy is profoundly conservative. It seeks not to fashion new modes of understanding out of their encounter with what Stowe calls "the outcast wanderer,"[21] but rather to reclothe that wanderer in the memorial vestments of their past, and so re-create the stranger in the image of their son. Dressing the slave as a little Henry, just as Tom Sawyer dresses up Jim in *Huckleberry Finn*, the Birds' sympathy preserves the logic of slavery by imposing on the other a shaping and artificial will. The slave is passive in this relation. Silent and unnamed in this exchange, Eliza's child is unable to resist a form of sympathy that restores him to tender but nonetheless coercive and predetermined modes of understanding. Re-dressed as Henry, the black slave becomes the figment of the Birds' imagination, a theme Ralph Ellison will explore in *Invisible Man*. He becomes the dream figure of their own dear son.

Whitman's sympathy replaces the fugitive slave with the fugitive soldier, but responds to an identical urge to reclaim, literally to reclothe in familiar forms, the lost children of the Civil War. And in this impulse we may read in part his debt to the sentimental novel. The social division of the body politic is imaged for Whitman in the radical strangeness of the afflicted body, the "brave boys . . . riddled with shot and shell," as Louisa May Alcott puts it.[22] The "riddling" of the male body represents a textual as well as a physical incoherence. To the extent that the nurse's writing reaffirms conventional values, she validates group meaning, closes the gap between herself and her reader, and wards off the disruptive presence of the unknown.

Whitman refamiliarizes the "riddled" body by repairing the bonds of affection threatened by death. He experiments with what Fisher terms a "politics of normality"[23]—the loaning out of full status and identity to figures who have been dehumanized by social conflict. In seeking to reconnect the afflicted soldier to shared patterns of meaning, Whitman's work takes shape as a conventional expression of the relation between self and other in his culture. Nursing civilizes forms of primary disorder and Whitman construes his role among the wounded as that of an almoner or missionary, a figure for this normalizing thematic. "I shall continue here in Washington . . . to work as a missionary, after my own style, among these hospitals," Whitman wrote in the Brooklyn *Eagle* in 1863, "for I find it in some respects curiously fascinating, with all its sadness."[24]

Crossing through Whitman's narratives are ghost soldiers who have lost the identifying signs of family, rank, background, and name: phantom children, who are, like the slaves in *Uncle Tom's Cabin*, outcasts from a familiar world: "One poor boy (this is a sample of one case out of the 600)," Whitman wrote his mother, describing the arrival in Washington of a trainload of wounded,

> he seemed to me quite young, he was quite small, (I looked at his
> body afterwards)—he groaned some as the stretcher-bearers were
> carrying him along—& again as they carried him through the hospi-
> tal gate, they set down the stretcher & examined him, & the poor
> boy was dead—they took him into the ward, & the doctor came
> immediately, but it was all of no use—the worst of it is too that he is
> entirely unknown—there was nothing on his clothes, or any one
> with him, to identify him—& he is altogether unknown—Mother, it
> is enough to rack one's heart.[25]

Virtually identical scenes punctuate the nursing narratives of the Civil War. Katharine Prescott Wormeley recounts this experience in a letter to her mother in 1862:

> One of them died this morning, unconscious, as usual, and so quietly
> that it was some minutes before I believed it, though Dr. Ware said
> it was so. He was speechless when he came into our hands,—sent
> down with no indication of name or regiment; and so he dies. There
> is another dying man lying next to where he lay; and though his eyes
> are bright and intelligent, he can give no sign, and I cannot discover
> anything about him. So many nameless men come down to us,
> speechless and dying, that now we write the names and regiments of

the bad cases and fasten them to their clothing, so that if they are speechless when they reach other hands, they may not die like dogs, and be buried in nameless graves, and remain forever "missing" to their friends.[26]

Anonymous and dehumanized, these vague strangers pose the threat remediated by sympathetic attention, as the nurse seeks to restore to a kind of ordinary humanness figures who are otherwise, as Whitman says, "entirely unknown." "D. S. G., bed 52, wants a good book; has a sore, weak throat; would like some horehound candy; is from New Jersey, 28th regiment," Whitman writes in a characteristic passage from *Specimen Days*. "C. H. L., 145th Pennsylvania, lies in bed 6, with jaundice and erysipelas; also wounded; stomach easily nauseated; bring him some oranges, also a little tart jelly." "J. H. G., bed 24, wants an undershirt, drawers, and socks" (p. 750). The socks, the candy, the gifts of money, clothing, and food: these objects are a kind of social badge in Whitman. They resignify the stranger's participation in communal practice and advertise his group identity and belonging. They are the tokens from Henry's bureau.

A TURN OF THE EYE OR HAND

Regardless of how deeply felt such acts of compassion were for Whitman, they suggest a relation between self and other that is, like the Birds', profoundly conservative. The recuperative sympathy of Whitman's "politics of normality" implies a coercion no less severe in its way than the refashioning of Eliza's son. Like the slave in Stowe's novel, Whitman's "dear boys" are passive, accommodating, and silent. They offer no resistance to forms of sympathy that restore them not only to familiar habits of relation but also to an ideological construction of Union they may or may not share.

Yet in poems like "Come Up from the Fields, Father" and "Vigil Strange I Kept on the Field One Night" Whitman is clearly aware of this conflict and offers as an alternative response to suffering, and a critique of his own method, a subject who refuses to participate in the sentimental reaffirmation of union. In "Come Up from the Fields, Father," for instance, Whitman shows how the effect of loss leads not to reparation but to a deeper withdrawal. The poem takes place as the mother's response to the death of her son in a Washington hospital, but this "universal" experience of grief—"Every family has directly or indirectly some representative"—remains for the mother specific and unconsoled.[27] The child is not a "representative" instance but an "only son"— "he is dead already; / The only son is dead."[28] Like Stowe, Whitman dramatizes the unexpected death of a beloved child, but unlike the death of Little Eva in *Uncle Tom's Cabin*, this death does not precipitate an "experiential equation" by which the mother's loss could be equated with others. As the mother renounces analogies for her experience, her grief becomes a source of profound disruption. Reversing Christian and sentimental traditions of typology, the mother will not give up the particularity of her "only son" and so signify his death as a sacrificial substitute for others, a representative in Whitman's Hospital Congress. Instead she withdraws from the substitutional logic of sentimentality, just as she withdraws from shared norms of social relation (sleeping, eating), and finally, in the poem's last lines, she withdraws as a figure of literary representation as well:

> By day her meals untouch'd—then at night fitfully sleeping, often
>   waking,
> In the midnight waking, weeping, longing with one deep longing,
> O that she might withdraw unnoticed—silent from life, escape and
>   withdraw,
> To follow, to seek, to be with her dear dead son.[29]

The mother refuses to be consoled. She refuses to be normalized, and her "fitful sleeping" contrasts the "calm, regular-breathing lethargy" of Whitman's typically pacified soldier.[30]

"Vigil Strange I Kept on the Field One Night" poses a similar critique of sentimental paradigms.[31] Just as the mother holds herself and her son back from the consolations of shared sympathy, the lover-poet refuses to embody his grief in the visible signs of loss. The "strangeness" of the vigil suggests a response to death that withholds rather than loans out such signs, and remains importantly eccentric to the normalizing rhythm of public ritual and shared meaning:

> Vigil strange I kept on the field one night,
> When you, my son and my comrade, dropt at my side that day,
> One look I but gave, which your dear eyes return'd, with a look I
>   shall never forget;
> One touch of your hand to mine, O boy, reach'd up as you lay on the
>   ground;
> Then onward I sped in the battle, the even-contested battle;
> Till late in the night reliev'd, to the place at last again I made my
>   way;
> Found you in death so cold, dear comrade—found your body, son of
>   responding kisses, (never again on earth responding;)
> Bared your face in the starlight—curious the scene—cool blew the
>   moderate night-wind;
> Long there and then in vigil I stood, dimly around me the battle-
>   field spreading;
> Vigil wondrous and vigil sweet, there in the fragrant silent night;
> But not a tear fell, not even a long-drawn sigh—Long, long I gazed;
> Then on the earth partially reclining, sat by your side, leaning my
>   chin in my hands;
> Passing sweet hours, immortal and mystic hours with you, dearest
>   comrade—Not a tear, not a word.[32]

Strikingly absent from the poem are the capitalized abstractions of other poems in *Drum-Taps*—"Democracy," "Columbia," "Libertab"— ideological constructs that would subsume the anomaly of the soldier's death and validate the prosecution of the war.[33] The poem is silent on those subjects, and its withholding, its "vigil of silence," guards against appropriating the soldier within overarching providential or historical designs. The poem disclaims that appropriation. It refuses to participate in the forgetfulness necessary to transform death into *exemplum*. Whitman often deploys a legitimating rhetoric of Union by which to repair the strangeness of the Civil War. But in this poem it is the preservation of that strangeness that interests the poet. The lover returns to reclaim the lost soldier, an act resonant with the paradigms of literary sentimentality, but what is being reclaimed precisely is not a public identity but a private relation, a wilderness relation indifferent to shared notions of loss. The poet's wordless grief—"not a tear fell, not even a long-drawn sigh"—refuses to embody itself in the sentimental rhetoric by which Whitman, in other moods, sought to regather the dead.

The severe abruptness of the poem's ending signals this discrepancy between public and private orders of meaning. As if to remind us that grief pursues its own pace, its own necessary rhythms, the sudden bump of the last line—"And buried him where he fell"—marks a point of detachment:

> Vigil for boy of responding kisses, (never again on earth
>   responding;)
> Vigil for comrade swiftly slain—vigil I never forget, how as day
>   brighten'd,
> I rose from the chill ground, and folded my soldier well in his
>   blanket,
> And buried him where he fell.[34]

The poet pushes off at this moment, not only from the corpse but also from the reader, as if to preserve lines of demarcation threatened by a sympathetic blur of compassion. Insofar as the poetic line seems incongruent, rhythmically and tonally odd, it evokes a felt moment of resistance to a regularizing pattern, a pattern and politics of normality that would round off the strangeness of the soldier's death and the poet's vigil.

Whitman's persona swings between antithetical roles, affirming, at times, the mutuality between self and other in poems like "Over the Carnage Rose Prophetic a Voice": "Be not dishearten'd—Affection shall solve the problems of Freedom"; yet, at other times renouncing that mutuality in cool assertions of difference. "Did you ask dulcet rhymes from me?" the poet asks:

> Did you find what I sang erewhile so hard to follow, to understand?
> Why I was not singing erewhile for you to follow, to understand—
>   nor am I now;
> —What to such as you, anyhow, such a poet as I?—therefore leave
>   my works,
> And go lull yourself with what you can understand.[35]

Imperious and defensive, Whitman's persona refuses to diminish the eccentricity of his war and equate his experience with anyone else's. Whitman's "go lull yourself" is a private declaration of independence, a sharp refusal of the rhymed regularity of a dulcet Union.

A quality of compassion that could remain both distant and near became an urgent psychological need for Whitman in the course of his work in the hospitals. Like Alcott's, Whitman's career as a Civil War nurse ended in emotional collapse, an experience that was caused, Whitman believed, by identifying too closely with the suffering of others. Well before his breakdown in June 1864, Whitman wrote his mother with an impending sense of this crisis: "Mother, I have had quite an attack of sore throat & distress in my head for some days past, up to last night. . . . I am told that I hover too much over the beds of the hospitals, with fever & putrid wounds."[36] A sense of obsessional "hovering" emerges often in Whitman's Civil War writings, and suggests a psychological context for the paradoxical quality of the poet's sympathy. "I cannot give up my Hospitals," Whitman wrote to his brother Thomas in 1863. "I never before had my feelings so thoroughly and (so far) permanently absorbed, to the very roots, as by these huge swarms of dear, wounded, sick, dying boys."[37]

Whitman's remark echoes a key phrase in his formulation of the role of the democratic writer. Feeling himself "absorbed" by the wounded, Whitman ironically confirmed what he had specified in 1855 as the very proof of the democratic poet: "The proof of a poet is that his country absorbs him as affectionately as he has absorbed it."[38] The psychic cost of this absorption, however, was the loss of inner distance and reserve on which Whitman's writing, indeed his own mental health, depended. "The Dresser" responds to this conflict. Oscillating between absorption and indifference, Whitman's wound-dresser acts out an embodied hesitation, an irregular rhythm of stopping and then moving on:

> An old man bending, I come, among new faces,
> Years looking backward, resuming, in answer to children,
> *Come tell us old man,* as from young men and maidens that love me;
> Years hence of these scenes, of these furious passions, these chances,
> Of unsurpass'd heroes, (was one side so brave? the other was equally
>   brave;)
> Now be witness again—paint the mightiest armies of earth;
> Of those armies so rapid, so wondrous, what saw you to tell us?
> What stays with you latest and deepest? of curious panics,
> Of hard-fought engagements, or sieges tremendous, what
>   deepest remains? . . .
>   . . . .
>
>   But in silence, in dream's projections,
> While the world of gain and appearance and mirth goes on,
> So soon what is over forgotten, and waves wash the imprints off the
>   sand,
> In nature's reverie sad, with hinged knees returning, I enter the
>   doors—(while for you up there,
> Whoever you are, follow me without noise, and be of strong heart.)
>
>   Bearing the bandages, water and sponge,
> Straight and swift to my wounded I go,
> Where they lie on the ground, after the battle brought in;
> Where their priceless blood reddens the grass, the ground;
> Or to the rows of the hospital tent, or under the roof'd hospital;
> To the long rows of cots, up and down, each side, I return;
> To each and all, one after another, I draw near—not one do I miss;
> An attendant follows, holding a tray—he carries a refuse pail,

Soon to be fill'd with clotted rags and blood, emptied, and fill'd
   again.

   I onward go, I stop,
With hinged knees and steady hand, to dress wounds;
I am firm with each—the pangs are sharp, yet unavoidable;
One turns to me his appealing eyes—(poor boy! I never knew you,
Yet I think I could not refuse this moment to die for you, if that
   would save you.)

   On, on I go—(open, doors of time! open, hospital doors!)
The crush'd head I dress, (poor crazed hand, tear not the bandage
   away;)
The neck of the cavalry-man, with the bullet through and through, I
   examine;
Hard the breathing rattles, quite glazed already the eye, yet life
   struggles hard;
(Come, sweet death! be persuaded, O beautiful death!
In mercy come quickly.)

   From the stump of the arm, the amputated hand,
I undo the clotted lint, remove the slough, wash off the matter and
   blood;
Back on his pillow the soldier bends, with curv'd neck, and side-
   falling head;
His eyes are closed, his face is pale, he dares not look on the bloody
   stump,
And has not yet looked on it.

.   .   .   .

   I am faithful, I do not give out;
The fractur'd thigh, the knee, the wound in the abdomen,
These and more I dress with impassive hand—(yet deep in my
   breast a fire, a burning flame.)[39]

The rhythm of motion and arrest in the poem—"I onward go, I stop,"
"On, on I go"—is the narrative pattern of Civil War lyrics like "Vigil
Strange I Kept on the Field One Night," "A March in the Ranks Hard-

Prest," and "As Toilsome I Wander'd": "Long, long I muse, then on my way go wandering." It is a rhythm that evokes improvisational, ad hoc instances of compassion in place of a consistent religious or philosophical point of view. Stopping and then moving on, the poem textualizes the makeshift shelters strung across the landscape of Whitman's war: the improvised hospitals of *Memoranda During the War*, the bivouacs and temporary campsites of *Drum-Taps*, the "Shebang" enclosures of his journal—shelters that provide a momentary stay against confusion but which offer no permanent anchorage against the uncertainty and drift of the war.

The catalogue of discontinuous contacts, as the poet turns from one soldier to another, allows Whitman to conceive as a quality of mercy the touch or glance in passing so important to the poetic innovation of *Leaves of Grass* as well as to his own psychic need for detachment and reserve. "Each case requires some peculiar adaptation to itself," Whitman wrote in a New York *Times* article. "A word, a friendly turn of the eye or touch of the hand in passing, if nothing more."[40] This image of sympathy as "turning"—a turn of the eye or hand—relates Whitman's dual roles as nurse and writer in "The Dresser." The turn or trope of poetic discourse, what Hayden White calls the "swerve" of poetic locution, implicates this logic of sympathy within the language of the poem itself.[41] Bending aside to a dying soldier, as does the poet-comrade in "A March in the Ranks Hard-Prest," bending down among new faces, as does the wound-dresser here—poet and poem are turned out from fixed alignments. They are inflected by the momentary awareness of others. Turning aside is the enabling possibility of the poetic for Whitman—its simplest and most fundamental definition—and what emerges then under the clarifying pressure of the war and its hospitals.

Imagined as a form of turning, moreover, Whitman's sympathy defends the poet from his own Medusa-like enchantment with death. The poet is pulled on and away from any single scene by the impinging awareness of others. What distinguishes sympathy from obsession is precisely this ability to turn away. And the wound-dresser seeks to preserve and elaborate a turn from fixed relations as the sign of poetic and psychic vitality. Attempting to turn out or move on from single attachments, the wound-dresser poses an alternative not only to the poet's own fixational Liebestod but to the rigid party and class alignments that had divided the nation as a whole and precipitated the crisis of the war.

Whitman builds this turn into his relation with the reader. The odd conflation of intimacy and distance in Whitman's address to the reader—"while for you up there, / Whoever you are, follow me without noise, and be of strong heart"—calls attention to the textuality of a mass-produced poem otherwise occluded by Whitman's more characteristic appeal to preverbal forms of sympathy, "the silent soothing of [the nurse's] presence" (p. 754). To the extent that Whitman makes prominent the textuality of the poem, his writing risks the fate of paper agreements misread and compromised by interpretation. But such writing, precisely as writing, makes possible a restorative address crucial to Whitman's understanding of democratic union. On the one hand, the poet is speaking directly to a single reader, a "you up there" bending over the upturned surface of his page. The poet's solicitude for this reader—"be of strong heart"—parallels the invigorating touch or glance of the wound-dresser himself. There is a sense of almost shocking intimacy at this moment, as the poet seems to open his eyes, look up from the page, and address a reader bending above him. Yet, in the same instant, this touch is diffused and depersonalized by our recognition that the poet addresses not a single reader but a mass public, a "you whoever you are." The intimacy of the single touch is turned suddenly into a form of relation capacious enough to reach all of America. And this sense of reach is inseparable from the technical innovations of a mass printing and distribution, innovations Whitman recognized and exploited from the beginning of his career.

The textuality Whitman works at times to efface as an obstacle to unanimity returns at such moments as a saving force of detachment, for the reader as well as the poet. The isolated self of a single reader is opened to a sense of alternatives by the indeterminacy of Whitman's "you whoever you are." The isolated self is opened, in other words, to that impinging awareness of others by which the poet signifies the experience of compassion. The printed poem is instrumental to that conception by allowing Whitman to affiliate a sense of otherness within his most intimate address, and thus to stir attention to forms of relation exceeding the autonomy of the isolated reader. As the textuality of the poem awakens us to that larger audience, that plural "you," it ministers as much to its readers as to its soldiers, and becomes both an instance and an enactment of Whitman's concept of sympathy.

Whitman exploits the tension between normative and disruptive models of compassion in his description of the Union soldier Thomas Haley in a passage from *Specimen Days*. In this passage, Whitman subsumes the anomaly of suffering within a familiar type and affirms the coherence of social and poetic union. At the same time, however, Whitman insinuates a complexity at odds with his own normalizing thematic, an extravagance exceeding the reparative terms of the text itself. As so often in Whitman, this extravagance is related to the drift of a homosexual erotic. Thomas Haley's description takes place in a chapter titled "Some Specimen Cases," in an autobiography titled *Specimen Days*. Whitman's titles call attention to the power of his writing to master and regularize the strangeness of experience, its power to reduce experience to an exemplary role—specimen instances of a higher law—and so preserve the unities put in question by the perturbations of war and love.[42]

> In one of the hospitals I find Thomas Haley, company M, 4th New York cavalry—a regular Irish boy, a fine specimen of youthful physical manliness—shot through the lungs—inevitably dying. . . . I saw Tom when first brought here, three days since, and didn't suppose he could live twelve hours—(yet he looks well enough in the face to a casual observer.) He lies there with his frame exposed above the waist, all naked, for coolness, a fine built man, the tan not yet bleach'd from his cheeks and neck. It is useless to talk to him, as with his sad hurt, and the stimulants they give him, and the utter strangeness of every object, face, furniture, &c., the poor fellow,

even when awake, is like some frighten'd, shy animal. Much of the time he sleeps, or half sleeps. (Sometimes I thought he knew more than he show'd.) I often come and sit by him in perfect silence; he will breathe for ten minutes as softly and evenly as a young babe asleep. Poor youth, so handsome, athletic, with profuse beautiful shining hair. One time as I sat looking at him while he lay asleep, he suddenly, without the least start, awaken'd, open'd his eyes, gave me a long steady look, turning his face very slightly to gaze easier—one long, clear, silent look.

(pp. 724–25)

If Jonathan Wallace, the Confederate soldier dying at Douglas Hospital, shows one side of Whitman's sympathy, Thomas Haley shows another. Despite his status as a type or specimen, "a regular Irish boy," there is something decidedly irregular about Whitman's description. Thomas Haley's complexity works against his easy assimilation by a "casual" reader or observer. And Whitman's parenthetical asides—("yet he looks"), ("Sometimes I thought")—point up a realm of meaning only partly disclosed by the paragraph's dominant voice. Whitman's passage encourages an apprehensive, gently skeptical sympathy restrained by a recognition of secrecy, hiddenness, and erotic depth.[43] The "profuse beautiful shining hair" in Whitman's description of Haley, a close equivalent of Hester's dark, abundant hair in *The Scarlet Letter*, evokes a relation exceeding the conventional roles of nurse and patient in Whitman, as it exceeds the conventional roles of minister and parishioner in Hawthorne. The sudden reversal of fixed roles, as the soldier awakens and looks back at his nurse-watcher, recovers that suspense as a characteristic of the writing. The fixed positions of observer and observed, subject and object, nurse and patient, give way in such moments to a relation of mutuality within which the self may play either part. And it is the surprise of this reversal, this sudden "turn," that Whitman seems most to cherish as the countersign to an imminent death. By displaying this unevenness in his hospital descriptions, Whitman stirs attention to an awakened vitality and interrupts, for a moment, the slow settling into sleep, indifference, and death.

There is "something odd about them," Whitman notes, describing "Spiritual Characters among the Soldiers" in *Memoranda During the War*. "Something veil'd and abstracted is often a part of the manners of these beings. . . . They are often young men, obeying the events and occasions about them, marching, soldiering, fighting . . . unaware of their own nature, (as to that, who is aware of his own nature?) their companions only understanding that they are different from the rest, more silent, 'something odd about them,' and apt to go off and meditate and muse in solitude."[44] As their musing suggests, such soldiers may be figures for the poet's sense of his own nature. In the list of alternative titles for his autobiography—a list that includes "Notes of a half-Paralytic," "Gossip at Early Candle-light," "Echoes and Escapades," "Sand-Drifts," "Drifts and Cumulus"—Whitman considered entitling his work simply "Oddments" (p. 886). And while ultimately affirming the typological coherence of the title "Specimen Days," Whitman nonetheless calls attention to what that coherence leaves out. And he preserves as a principal value in the autobiography the unsettling of proprietary categories by erotic and semiotic drift, the oddments of an unsorted imagination.

The uneasiness of Whitman's metaphors for Thomas Haley (a shy animal, a young babe, an athletic youth) presents a confounding of categories that staves off his fixed nomination as a "specimen case." Thomas Haley evokes, like the autobiography, multiple titles. The copper pennies placed over the eyes of the corpse in Whitman's representations of death—"a corpse of a poor soldier, just dead, of typhoid fever. The attendants had just straighten'd the limbs, put coppers on the eyes, and were laying it out" (p. 774)—emblematize a figure who can no longer turn out from or reverse its classification, a soldier who can no longer look back. Cashed in for the uniformity of money, the corpse represents an evenness in contrast to the suspense of the living body, the odd vitality of "Thomas Haley."

According to Jane Tompkins, "sentimental novels take place, meta-phorically and literally, in the 'closet.'" Whitman anticipates and builds on this idea. He adapts the closet politics of the sentimental novel to his own interests as a gay writer and nurse, just as he adapts the sexual secret of the heterosexual romance to a theory of political representation based on gay love. The sentimental impulse willing to erase the eccentricity of its subject is countered in scenes like these by what Thoreau calls an "expeditious" compassion willing to suspend fixed assumptions and enter with care into a realm of uncertain value.[45] Such passages do not recuperate the stranger. They do not cure or calm anything. Whitman's desire to repair the intelligibility of experience as a Civil War writer is offset by an equally urgent need to maintain the strangeness of a self held back from full disclosure, a self that exceeds the terms of its appear-ance with the promise and possibility of something more: "I thought he knew more than he show'd."

In the sentimental tradition of Harriet Beecher Stowe, Whitman dis-covered a normalizing discourse of literary sympathy. He discovered a sympathy that could transform riddled bodies into fair specimens, out-cast wanderers into favored sons. Writing as both a national and a homosexual poet, however, Whitman tempers that sympathy with a gay mistrust skeptical of normalizing ritual and alert to the paradoxically distancing turns of compassion. Whitman, too, knows more than he shows, and he builds that extravagance, the extra-text of the gay closet, into the writing and role of the wound-dresser. Preserving the romance of a body incompletely subsumed within fixed categories—incompletely "straighten'd"—Whitman promotes a quality of love that both invites and resists the settled determination of the other.

FOUR

Telling It Slant
Medical Representation
in Memoranda During the War

Nineteenth-century medicine was haunted by that absolute eye
that cadaverizes life and rediscovers in the corpse the frail,
broken nervure of life.

Michel Foucault, The Birth of the Clinic

In January 1874, Whitman published six autobiographical narratives in
the New York *Weekly Graphic* titled "'Tis But Ten Years Since." Collected
and republished in 1875 as *Memoranda During the War*, these sketches
were the culmination of a project Whitman had been considering for
several years. In 1863 Whitman outlined the plans for two books on the
Civil War hospitals—"Hours in Our Military Hospitals" and "Memoranda of a Year"[1]—both of which were left unpublished. Also unfinished
was Whitman's plan to write the regimental history of the Fifty-first New
York, the regiment in which his brother George had served during the
war. The most ambitious project of this period, however, was Whitman's
plan to write a comprehensive Civil War narrative—"the History of the
War in a great volume or several volumes"[2]—that would fuse social,
political, and military experience into a single whole. This grand history

95

would lay the foundation for a revolutionary change in American literature and become the source text for a regenerate and reunified postwar American culture.

Memoranda During the War is not that book. Instead, reversing the ambitions of such a narrative, Whitman disclaims the authority—even the possibility—of a comprehensive Civil War history. The "interior history" of the war, Whitman announces at the beginning of the *Memoranda*, "will never be written—perhaps must not and should not be":

> Such was the War. It was not a quadrille in a ball-room. Its interior history will not only never be written, its practicality, minutia of deeds and passions, will never be even suggested. The actual Soldier of 1862–'65, North and South, with all his ways, his incredible dauntlessness, habits, practices, tastes, language, his appetite, rankness, his superb strength and animality, lawless gait, and a hundred unnamed lights and shades of camp—I say, will never be written— perhaps must not and should not be.[3]

Why must the war not be written? Why does Whitman take pains to renounce the authority of his text and insist on the discrepancy between the war and its representation? The Civil War is, after all, written in the *Memoranda*, and its scenes suggest at least something of the war's meaning. Furthermore, although Whitman insists on the political value of the *Memoranda*, it is unclear how a text that puts in question the validity of representation can be serviceable to a democratic polity dependent on a similar claim. On the contrary, the failure of literary representation thematized in the opening of the *Memoranda* would suggest a specific episode in the larger breakdown of representational politics surrounding the Civil War, and Whitman's text would sustain rather than repair that loss.

Putting in question the possibility of representative narrative, Whitman responds to widespread changes in American life taking place in the "ten years since" the war. In particular, the *Memoranda* responds to an increasing cultural and political centralization that violated, Whitman believed, the democratic meaning of the war. At the end of the *Memoranda* Whitman argues that the war was caused not by slavery but by a monopolistic usurpation of power that victimized working people on both sides of the line. The threat to this artisan class was the consolidation of power by a political elite, a consolidation strengthened rather than restrained by the experience of the Civil War. In response to this consolidation, Whitman disclaims the sufficiency of representation as a largely negative attempt to free American democracy from the deforming terms of its present appearance. Whitman's aspiration for a democratic republic of free labor was defeated after the Civil War by the rapid rise of an industrialized power-state, what he called the "leviathan" of Gilded Age America. "Pride, competition, segregation, vicious wilfulness, and license beyond example, brood already upon us," Whitman wrote four years earlier in *Democratic Vistas*. "Unwieldy and immense, who shall hold in behemoth? who bridle leviathan?"[4] By insisting that a comprehensive history of the Civil War has not been and cannot be written, Whitman undermines the ideological foundations of this leviathan and presents his own "impromptu jottings" (p. 3) as a decentralized, individualistic, and democratic alternative.

I SAW ASKANT THE ARMIES

In *The Unwritten War*, Daniel Aaron relates the manifold drive toward centralization in postwar America to the emergence of a new style of writing: the disciplined and efficient prose of the veteran soldier. "New conditions also required a new style of writing," Aaron explains, "one commensurate with the practical requirements of the nation. . . . Writers in post-War America were now urged to cultivate a soldierly or businesslike style."[5] In his essay "Caesar's Art of War and of Writing," the Connecticut novelist and soldier John De Forest identifies Caesar's *Commentaries* as the model of this soldierly style. The discipline of a well-fought war and the directness of a well-made sentence correspond in De Forest's argument. And it is for him richly significant that a nation's best soldiers—Caesar, Napoleon, Wellington, and, many would soon add, Ulysses S. Grant—were also its best writers. The social and racial consolidation of Caesar's conquests—his power to "thrash and crush" the Gauls—provided the foundation for a literary style hating excess and devoted to "[e]xtreme simplicity."[6] Literary and political consolidation reinforce one another in Caesar's *Commentaries*, and the Civil War provided an identical chastening to the social and literary insubordinations of America. Although written in 1879, De Forest's essay draws on a theme in American literature developing since the war. For many writers the Civil War made possible "a centralization of thoughts, feelings, and views on national subjects,"[7] a centralization enthusiastically supported by such writers as Edmund Clarence Stedman, Thomas Bailey Aldrich, Richard Henry Stoddard, James Russell Lowell, and, perhaps most surprisingly, Emerson himself.[8]

Whitman deflects and complicates the arts of war and writing. He does not see war directly, as Caesar does, but mediately, obliquely, in glimpses: "The present Memoranda may furnish a few stray glimpses into that life, and into those lurid interiors of the period, never to be fully convey'd to the future" (p. 5). In the climactic recovery of poetic vision in section 15 of "When Lilacs Last in the Dooryard Bloom'd," the poet's sight, though "unclosed," remains glancing:

> Loud in the pines and cedars dim,
> Clear in the freshness moist and the swamp-perfume,
> And I with my comrades there in the night.
>
> While my sight that was bound in my eyes unclosed,
> As to long panoramas of visions.
> And I saw askant the armies.[9]

Seeing "askant," Whitman demonstrates an alternative to the fronting of political, medical, and literary centrism dominating American culture after the war. Turning aside the assurance of authoritative control—exposing what is left out by that control—Whitman challenges the epistemological assumptions of imperial history as well as the social consolidations that history supports. Against such consolidation, Whitman will emphasize the elusiveness of the "real war" and he will insist on his inability to contain or stabilize its meanings.[10] This is a political as much as a literary issue for Whitman, as it is also for De Forest. Prodigal, clannish, poetic, "the very Irish of to-day"[11]—the Gauls are clarified by imperial power, simplified as much by Caesar's sentences as by his legions. And it is this simplification that concerns Whitman in his writings on the war.

In the most violent political rhetoric of his late career, Whitman insists that the Civil War had changed little in American culture, and that its real issues, like its dead, remain unreckoned:

> I say that the sixteenth, seventeenth and eighteenth terms of the American Presidency have shown that the villainy and shallowness of rulers (back'd by the machinery of great parties) are just as eligible to These States as to any foreign despotism, kingdom, or empire— there is not a bit of difference. History is to record those three Presidentiads, and especially the administrations of Fillmore and Buchanan, as so far our topmost warning and shame. Never were publicly display'd more deform'd, mediocre, snivelling, unreliable, false-hearted men! Never were These States so insulted, and attempted to be betray'd! All the main purposes for which the government was establish'd, were openly denied. . . . (The Slavery contest is settled—and the War is over—yet do not those putrid conditions, too many of them, still exist? still result in diseases, fevers, wounds—not of War and Army Hospitals— but the wounds and diseases of Peace?)

(p. 64)

It is not difficult to imagine what Whitman meant by the "wounds and diseases of Peace" in 1875. The history of American Reconstruction is a history of censorship, bureaucratization, and political scandal— some of which touched Whitman himself. After the war the poet became the object of what he called "two or three pretty serious special official buffetings."[12] Whitman was fired from the Interior Department in 1865, and sixteen years later *Leaves of Grass* was banned as an obscene book. The voices of Comstockery and repression did not speak for America, Whitman had to believe. Discounting their authority, Whitman sought to distinguish the latent character of an unexpressed America from the external and repellent evidence of its disease.[13] This idea was so important to Whitman that he staked the meaning of the war itself on its validity:

> To me, the points illustrating the latent Personal Character and eligibilities of These States . . . were of more significance even than the Political interests involved. (As so much of a Race depends on what it thinks of death, and how it stands personal anguish and sickness. As, in the glints of emotions under emergencies, and the indirect traits and asides in Plutarch, &c., we get far profounder clues to the antique world than all its more formal history).
>
> *(pp. 4–5)*

This theory of latency, as well as the Plutarch example, are taken from Emerson's essay "Character." The "undemonstrable force" of character, Emerson explains, remains creatively unequal to the visible signs of its publication:

> I have read that those who listened to Lord Chatham felt that there was something finer in the man, than anything which he said. It has been complained of our brilliant English historian of the French Revolution, that when he has told all his facts about Mirabeau, they do not justify his estimate of his genius. The Gracchi, Agis, Cleomenes, and others of Plutarch's heroes, do not in the record of facts equal their own fame. Sir Philip Sidney, the Earl of Essex, Sir Walter Raleigh, are men of great figure, and of few deeds. We cannot find the smallest part of the personal weight of Washington, in the narrative of his exploits. The authority of the name of Schiller is too great for his books. . . . [B]ut somewhat resided in these men which begot

an expectation that outran all their performance. The largest part of their power was latent. This is that which we call Character,—a reserved force which acts directly by presence, and without means. It is conceived of as a certain undemonstrable force, a Familiar or Genius, by whose impulses the man is guided, but whose counsels he cannot impart.[14]

This idea had inspired Whitman in the 1840s with the hope that his own poetic genius was not limited by the hard evidence of its accomplishments: "The Inca's Daughter," "The Spanish Lady," "Ambition," and so on. As Jerome Loving has argued, Emerson made it possible to believe that these works were inadequate signs—"faint clews & indirections"—of a genuine but undemonstrable poetic character, a real Whitman still simmering.[15] This theory freed the poet to believe in an open future, a future determined neither by the limitations of Whitman's family and social class nor by the mediocrity of his own published work. And it is to this idea that Whitman turns in his representation of the war. The published evidence of the war—the textual and social record of the Gilded Age—is also a distorted indication of an unseen presence, a real America yet to emerge.

The elusiveness of the real thus becomes one of the *Memoranda's* most urgent themes:

> Of scenes like these, I say, who writes—who e'er can write, the story? Of many a score—aye, thousands, North and South, of unwrit heroes, unknown heroisms, incredible, impromptu, first-class desperations—who tells? No history, ever—No poem sings, nor music sounds, those bravest men of all—those deeds. No formal General's report, nor print, nor book in the library, nor column in the paper, embalms the bravest, North or South, East or West. Unnamed, unknown, remain, and still remain, the bravest soldiers.
>
> *(p. 16)*

Unable to contain these heroes—unable to "cast" them in bloodless type or "embalm" them in preserving fluid—Whitman clears the way for a living history different from its transcription. The story of the war exceeds its representation in the same way Agis's heroism or Lord Chatham's eloquence or Washington's character are unaccounted for within the narrative of their exploits. Too great for his books, Schiller's name survives its casting in text and what remains—an "undemonstrable force"—undermines the closure of his account.

Acting on this idea, Whitman presents the hospital as a series of incomplete views. We do not see the body directly in this work but obliquely—"askant"—and Whitman insists in this way on the discrepancy between the fullness of his subject and the incompleteness of its presentation. As in the "Calamus" settings, Whitman's hospital is a space of intimate glances that calls attention to the limits rather than the vista of our vision. The body is withheld in both settings, screened by an obstructive narrative or poetic presence. In "Calamus" this withholding creates a textual erotic deferring the disclosure of final meanings. "Come I am determin'd to unbare this broad breast of mine," the poet promises in "Scented Herbage of My Breast." "Emblematic and capricious blades I leave you, now you serve me not, / I will say what I have to say by itself."[16] By offering, and then withholding, the poetic body—"this broad breast of mine"—Whitman plays on a reader's desire to strip off the obstructive blades of language and possess the poem's real meaning unadorned. The "Calamus" poems, like the *Memoranda*, allude to final disclosures—a "real reality," an "interior history"[17]—neither text is willing to provide. Instead Whitman elaborates a complex apparatus of obstruction—screens, baffles, interstices, veils—interposed between his readers and what they see.[18] These obstacles are the instruments of a living vitality, what Whitman calls the "vital play and significance" of an unmastered subject (p. 24). The reader's partial apprehension of the text corresponds to the waywardness of that subject, a body glimpsed—"a glimpse through an interstice caught," "cought glimpses of him through the open door"—but never fully mastered or possessed.[19] Because vision is insistently reductive, it cannot claim to exhaust the complexity of its field and so remains subject to—even encourages—difference, revision, and critique. By means of this uncertainty, Whitman sustains a "living heat and excitement" lost not only in the reification of writing but also in the deanimation of suffering, the simplification of a complex self by hunger, cholera, dysentery, or pain.

More than a specific place or practice, medicine is a mode of perception for Whitman, a way of seeing—and not seeing—the body. This is an idea Foucault explores in *The Birth of the Clinic*, a work that helps illustrate, by contrast, Whitman's view of medicine. Like Whitman, Foucault takes as his subject the intersection of body and gaze as he describes a subtle shift in the ways patients were seen by doctors at the end of the eighteenth century. In the Paris clinics of Bichat, Laennec, Bayle, and Pinel, a sick or injured person became a "case" or "specimen"—not a person with an illness but an illness seen through a person. This transformation was both subtle and decisive. The French pathologists sought to see affliction in isolation from the patient himself, abstracting the disease from its local occurrence—the body of this or that person—in order to compare it with other patients suffering the same distress.

Many Civil War physicians welcomed this transformation. According to Richard Shryock,

> A less fortunate aspect of [American] medical thought at midcentury
> was its emphasis upon specific diseases rather than—as in earlier
> days—on the general state of the patient's "system." This emphasis
> upon specificity pointed toward the identification of particular ill-
> nesses, and how discover causes or cures until diseases themselves
> were first known? But, meantime, inquiring physicians became more
> interested in diseases or in injuries as such than in the patients who
> harbored them.[20]

This way of seeing emerges often in accounts of Civil War nursing. Louisa May Alcott, for instance, describes a Washington surgeon who "had acquired a somewhat trying habit of regarding a man and his wound as separate institutions."[21] It is this habit of perception that Foucault traces in *The Birth of the Clinic*.

What is at stake in this transformation is medical certainty. Medicine cannot measure or define human beings. It cannot know a person with any degree of precision. But it can know disease. It can know and predict the course of cholera, dysentery, or pneumonia, but only if the physician can abstract the disease from the person, and so treat the patient—literally see the patient—as a case or type, the local instance of a pathological law understood, finally, in autopsy. What medicine knows it learns from the corpse. "That which hides and envelops, the curtain of night over truth, is, paradoxically, life," Foucault writes; "and death, on the contrary, opens up to the light of day the black coffer of the body."[22] What is obscure or confusing in the living body becomes clear in autopsy. What is "buried in the patient . . . like a cryptogram" becomes legible in dissection. Thus "living night is dissipated in the brightness of death." Thus death opens "the black coffer of the body." "[S]een in relation to death," Foucault says, "disease becomes exhaustively legible, open without remainder to the sovereign dissection of language and of the gaze."[23]

Modern medicine begins in these moments. Its birthplace is the autopsy theater and its conceptual origin is pathological anatomy. To know is to objectify and deaden. To know is to "open up a few bodies" and realize directly the hidden truth of disease. As Foucault seeks to master that fact he shows the crucial importance to medicine of the pathologist's case study. And he finds in that case study the same will to know—the same impulse toward totalitarian control—he uncovers in other institutions of the modern state: prisons, schools, asylums, factories. The goal of medical knowledge is unobstructed vision, Foucault argues, "the unobstructed transparency of the pathological being."[24] And with this insight, we sense medicine's place in Foucault's grim story of power. The modern clinic, it turns out, is another Panopticon, another branch in the capillary power of the state, another way of knowing bodies in order to tame and control them.

Like Foucault, Whitman emphasizes a deeply rooted convergence between politics and medicine but he understands the basis of that convergence differently. In place of the sovereign gaze, Whitman offers sketches and hints. In place of "unobstructed transparency," he offers screens and veils. In place of anatomic-clinical discourse, he offers a romance of surgery and medicine. Whitman's medical descriptions are deliberately angled, biased, off-center—queer. He sees his hospitals "askant," and he affirms the value in both medicine and democracy of what John Rawls calls a "veil of ignorance" in systems of power—self-conscious limits to what one can know, control, manage, or predict.[25] Like many Civil War nurses, Whitman resists totalitarian medicine in the same way he resists totalitarian politics. Both forms of authority are based on the same premise: the claim to see and know directly, the claim to certain knowledge. Whitman undermines that assurance. He loosens medical power by cherishing a conceptual play at odds with the dead certainty of the corpse. He explores an erotics of knowledge rather than a dissection, a gay flirtation rather than a dead embrace.

Clara Barton sought to cope with the anonymity of the Civil War hospitals by imagining her patients as children from her schoolrooms.[26] In this way she responded to the dehumanization of mass medicine, what was indeed "state medicine" in the army hospitals of the Civil War. Whitman copes with this threat differently. He restores human complexity to the soldiers he treats by seeing them not as cases but as comrades, gay friends and lovers who are never fully known, seen, objectified, or made public. "Something veil'd and abstracted is often a part of the manners of these beings," he says of hospitalized soldiers (p. 27). Whitman understood the ethical force of his writing in these terms: not as the stripping away of veils but as their recovery, not as a way of dissipating suspense but as a way of deepening and prolonging it. "And as for our future," Nietzsche writes in *The Gay Science*, "one will hardly find us again on the paths of those [who] want by all means to unveil, uncover, and put into a bright light whatever is kept concealed for good reasons. . . . We no longer believe that truth remains truth when the veils are withdrawn."[27]

In practice, this idea leads Whitman to cover the male body in a tissue of surfaces that both invites and obstructs a reader's will to know. The wound-dressing occurs not as a single surface but as a sequence of folds or layers enveloping the afflicted body and literally hiding it from sight. The covering fabric of the bandage or dressing is repeated at a series of intervals moving out from the body itself. It is repeated, for instance, in the pages of the poet's notebook held against the soldier's skin and "blotch'd here and there with more than one blood-stain" (p. 3). It is repeated once more in the "drapery of white curtains" hung above and around the soldier's cot (p. 22); then again in the expansive covering cloth of the hospital tent (p. 20); and then, finally, in "the melancholy, draper-ied night above, around" (p. 15). Whitman's "draperied night" sustains, and infinitely extends, the densely woven work of shelter.[28]

"That which hides and envelops, the curtain of night over truth, is, paradoxically, life," Foucault says. Whitman's *Memoranda* explores that paradox. His medical scenes are marked by what they hide as well as what they show: a "real war" he will not write, an "interior history" he will not reveal, the "full details" of a subject he will not disclose (p. 13). Whitman's most urgent meanings are unexpressed, or only partly expressed. And the mode of knowledge in his clinic is not the gaze but the glimpse, a partial view obscured by smoke, haze, crape, gauze, dark-ness, terror, or love: "just a glimpse," he says, just "a moment's look" (p. 13). Rejecting what Foucault calls "the absolute eye" of nineteenth-century medicine,[29] Whitman develops a mode of vision alert to the lim-its of its own perspective. The wounded body is never seen openly or exhaustively in Whitman's scenes. Instead the poet stands as a mediating screen between the reader and the body, restricting the range of vision and selecting the objects of attention. "Look at the fine large frames," he says (p. 11). "Notice that water-pail by the side of the bed" (p. 25). The reader's vision is held in check by this intermediate presence, a narrative obstruction that will not stand aside. "As you pass by," Whitman writes, inscribing a sense of slant or deflection into the act of reading itself, "[a]s you pass by, you must be on your guard where you look. I saw the other day a gentleman, a visitor apparently from curiosity, in one of the Wards, stop and turn a moment to look at an awful wound they were probing, &c. He turn'd pale, and in a moment more he had fainted away and fallen on the floor" (pp. 18–19).[30]

This is not the "unobstructed transparency of the pathological being." This is not "the sovereign dissection of language and of the gaze."[31] "If the capacity for unimpeded vision has been at the core of the biomedical sciences," Ludmilla Jordanova writes in *Sexual Visions*, "then we should be especially attentive to what were perceived as the obstacles in its way."[32] Whitman compels his readers to note those obstacles. By restoring an awareness of restraint in vision—"you must be on your guard where you look"—Whitman resists the despotism of unobstructed authority and explores a different mode of medical attention and care. The presence of textual obstructions—like the professional restraints built into the doctor-patient relationship—limit how the body can be looked at, how it can be approached, and what can be done to it. By writing these restraints into his representations of the body, Whitman seeks to recover the sense of limit erased by the wholesale death and violation of the war. Unlike the hospital, the battlefield offers indiscriminate access to the body. It is that place where the body can be seen and touched without restraint. Nurse and physician are granted intimate access to and knowledge of the body, but this access is presented as a desirable alternative to the unrestricted trespass of the war.

This withholding of the body allowed Whitman to construe as socially valuable the uncertainty of his own sexuality. Dismissing Whitman's claim that his hospital experiences were fundamentally democratic, much critical commentary simplifies Whitman's hospital career by reading it as an instance of homosexual sublimation. "He was less tormented by his homosexual leanings," Roger Asselineau writes, "which his visits to the hospitals permitted him to satisfy in part without incurring social disapproval or even suspicion. . . . He was undoubtedly motivated by charity, but, unconsciously at least, he was also moved by his desire and his need to be among young men."[33] By diverting sexual energy into socially sanctioned channels, nursing became the legitimate substitute for homosexual pleasure. Whitman's alleged desire for that legitimation—"He wanted to become manful, expansive, and normal"[34]—committed the poet to an unconscious masking of his love for soldiers like Lewy Brown and Thomas Sawyer. The signs of obliquity in the *Memoranda*—Whitman's "homosexual leanings"—thus suggest the poet's difference from a "normal" writer, Caesar perhaps, who could take his sex and his war straight.[35]

Rather than suggesting the unconscious mechanisms of sublimation—"unconsciously at least, he was also moved by his desire and his need to be among young men"—the screenings of the *Memoranda* are clearly deliberate. "See that screen there" (p. 25), Whitman says, as if the obstructions of his text could become synonymous with the healing protection of medical care. The evasiveness Asselineau and others adduce as evidence of a deficient and dangerous homosexual sublimation is in fact the means by which the suffering body regains a sense of privacy and with that privacy a sense of humanness itself. The hospital, Whitman claimed, is a "medium world"—a middle ground of artifactual and linguistic mediation that restores a protective, humanizing margin between the body and the world. The "furtiveness" of Whitman's sexuality—"There is something in my nature *furtive* like an old hen!" he once remarked[36]—takes shape as a desire to restore protective limits around a body at risk in the dehumanizing exposures of war.

Seeing directly is the principal issue not only in Asselineau's account of the *Memoranda* as sublimation but also in Timothy Sweet's account of the *Memoranda* as ideology. The evasiveness of Whitman's text is the means by which the poet dehistoricizes the Civil War, Sweet claims, and produces a monolithic and uncritical ideology of Union. Interdicting realistic analysis, ignoring the subjective mediation of vision, elaborating a depoliticized conception of nature, Whitman suppresses the "real war," Sweet claims, for the sake of ideological closure and legitimation.[37] One wonders of course why Whitman would want to legitimate a political situation he describes as "putrid" and "disease[d]" (p. 64). Nor is it clear how Whitman's indictment of American politics—"office-holders, office-seekers, pimps, malignants, conspirators, murderers, fancy-men" (p. 64)—can be read as an "idyllic ideology" that leaves "no space for politics."[38] Nevertheless, Sweet charges that by failing to see and write the "real war," Whitman rationalizes violence and neglects "the moral burden of representing repulsive events."[39]

Why is the representation of "repulsive events" a "moral burden"—particularly in a culture in which the unflinching apprehension of violence was a key issue in the construction of gender?[40] Is Ishmael's evasiveness equally suspect? And do we then see as morally superior Ahab's desire to confront evil directly or Chillingworth's obsession with uncovering the truth or Caesar's will to see only the facts? We can easily imagine medical representations in which seeing directly is itself a kind of violence. In Poe's "The Murders in the Rue Morgue," for example, the physician's medical report on the women's disfigured bodies perpetuates the sense of transgression. As the medical report lingers on the details of each wound—the throat, the chin, the tongue, the eyes—the women's bodies are laid open in a way that prolongs and elaborates the violence of the crime.[41] Unlike Whitman's fainting spectator, Poe's reader remains immune and privatized, free to study the probing of each wound, free to see directly.

As if in response to the transgressive violence of vision, many Civil War nursing narratives disclaim direct representations of suffering. "Most happy shall I be to escort you . . . into the 'horrors of hospital life,'" an anonymous nurse writes in *Notes of Hospital Life*. But, she warns, "[y]ou shall not see an open wound if I can help it."[42] Withholding the body of the wounded soldier is an explicitly moral burden in the nurse's narrative. Like Whitman, she presents the texture of her prose as a supplement to the wound dressings on the body itself. The exposure of the wounded soldier elicits not only the fabric of bandage and dressing but also the fabrication of the nurse's writing, a writing that in its twists and puns and euphemisms calls attention to itself as a surface interposed between the sufferer and the public world—an artificial margin, what John Hawkes calls a "second skin." In the self-conscious checks and balances of this style the writer poses an alternative to the unmediated violence of the war and the unobstructed vision of her reader.

NOTES LEFT OVER

Calling attention to what her readers will not see, the nurse anticipates the indirection of the *Memoranda*. But Whitman takes this idea a step further. Whitman's attempt to make his hospital material available to his reader is consistently imagined as a problem of citation, a problem of what to quote and what to leave out: "Of course there are among these thousands of prostrated soldiers in hospital here, all sorts of individual cases. On recurring to my note-book, I am puzzled which cases to select to illustrate the average of these young men and their experiences."[43] As a partial quotation, the text corresponds with the diminishment of the soldier himself, a figure who is also imagined as a quotation, a "fragmentary excerpt": "To-day as I was walking a mile or two south of Alexandria, I fell in with several large squads of the returning Western army . . . about a thousand in all, the largest portion of them half sick, some convalescents, &c. These fragmentary excerpts . . . I mark'd with curiosity, and talk'd with off and on for over an hour" (p. 51).

Consider how Whitman develops the analogy between text and body in this passage, referring to the soldiers as "fragmentary excerpts" in a way that recalls his descriptions of his own published jottings, the "scraps" of the *Memoranda* itself (p. 63). On the one hand, this seems consistent with Whitman's attempt to "textualize" the body in poems like "So Long" and "A Song for Occupations." But in this instance Whitman stresses the partializing nature of both textuality and embodiment. He calls attention to the difference between the unrealized plenitude of his subject—in this case, the invalid soldier—and the inadequacy of his publication in a fragmented text and an injured body. We do

not know the whole story, such passages suggest. We do not see or comprehend subjects inadequately represented by the bodies and books in
which they appear. The identity of the injured soldier exceeds the limits
of his body in the same way the meaning of the war bursts the admittedly
reductive bonds of Whitman's art. Both body and text are excerpts, quotations from larger wholes. Whitman thus recomposes as a medical and
literary issue the premise of his political idealism: the power of democracy to transcend the terms of its historical appearance or publication.
Just as the afflicted soldier calls attention to the difference between body
and self, and just as Whitman's quotations call attention to the difference
between text and subject, the political and social reality of a postwar
America Whitman found deeply distressing calls attention to the inadequate incarnation of democracy itself. Like the afflicted soldier, democracy is insufficiently or incompletely embodied. It escapes or evades the
defining attachment of historical circumstance—it exceeds that circumstance—and so preserves the promise of change. Body, text, and nation
still remained after the war—and this was the source of Whitman's hope
as a democratic writer—incomplete.

Whitman puts it this way in *Democratic Vistas:* "Then, as towards our
thought's finalè, (and, in that, overarching the true scholar's lesson,) we
have to say that there can be no complete or epical presentation of
democracy in the aggregate, or anything like it, at this day, because its
doctrines will only be effectually incarnated in any one branch, when, in
all, their spirit is at the root and centre."[44] It is an important concession.
Whitman had attempted nothing less than an "epical presentation of
democracy" in 1855. Containing multitudes, "Song of Myself" is, if
nothing else, a native epic meant to rival the classical tradition of Virgil's
Aeneid as well as the Christian tradition of Milton's *Paradise Lost*.[45]
Relinquishing that ambition, Whitman cultivates a self-conscious
incompleteness in his Civil War writings. He renounces any claim to
representative plenitude: any hope of composing a comprehensive
history, any desire to author full-bodied poems. Turning from what
Kenneth Burke calls "the *pleroma*"—the sense of "entrancing humane

fullness" in the early *Leaves of Grass*—Whitman now sees and writes in pieces, in "fragmentary excerpts."[46]

This is the principal shift in Whitman's late career, the principal difference in his writings before and after the war. But this change is not confined to Whitman's prose. Well before the *Memoranda*, in the Civil War poem "Give Me the Splendid Silent Sun," for example, Whitman dramatized this shift as a turning point in his art. The poem begins by evoking precisely that plenitude, that "entrancing" "fullness," so important to the epic ambitions of the early *Leaves of Grass:*

> Give me the splendid silent sun, with all his beams full-dazzling;
> Give me juicy autumnal fruit, ripe and red from the orchard;
> Give me a field where the unmow'd grass grows;
> Give me an arbor, give me the trellis'd grape;
> Give me fresh corn and wheat—give me serene-moving animals,
>   teaching content;
> Give me nights perfectly quiet, as on high plateaus west of the
>   Mississippi, and I looking up at the stars;
> Give me odorous at sunrise a garden of beautiful flowers, where I
>   can walk undisturb'd;
> Give me for marriage a sweet-breath'd woman, of whom I should
>   never tire;
> Give me a perfect child—give me, away, aside from the noise of the
>   world, a rural domestic life.[47]

We have seen much of this before: the sun-lit field in "A Farm Picture," the night stars in "When I Heard the Learn'd Astronomer," the "splendid silent sun" in the great crisis poems of the 1850s. This is a space of full presence, a space untouched by war and representation where objects emerge in their fullness, "beams full-dazzling." The autumnal apple remains "ripe and red from the orchard," for the poet has not yet eaten from that tree and his world remains unfallen, untroubled by the knowledge of partial things. If this is a prewar paradise, a prelapsarian garden, it is necessarily a heterosexual garden as well, a garden before the fall into homosexual knowledge. Once again the poet turns aside from the noise and clank of the world, as he did in "Calamus." But he no longer sings songs of "manly attachment" in that retreat but songs of marriage and children. The mutability of gay desire is banished from this garden. The poet no longer endures the stress of wounded lovers passing through his life. He no longer suffers from the impermanence of a homosexual erotic that does not settle into a quiet, plain way of living. For these lines at least, Whitman allows himself to imagine that quiet living, that perfect settlement. He allows himself to relax the negative capability of the war and its hospitals and achieve a sexual relation without loss or change, a wife "of whom I should never tire." This is indeed a love "[f]ast-anchor'd" and "eternal."[48]

Such certainties belong to some other poet, Whitman realizes, a pastoral poet far from the urban hospitals, a heterosexual poet far from the knowledge of "Calamus." Claiming that knowledge in the second half of the poem—"(O I see what I sought to escape, confronting, reversing my cries; / I see my own soul trampling down what it ask'd for")—the poet comes to terms with the partial fulfillments of a divided world:[49]

> Keep your splendid silent sun;
> Keep your woods, O Nature, and the quiet places by the woods;
> Keep your fields of clover and timothy, and your cornfields and
>   orchards;
> Keep the blossoming buckwheat fields, where the Ninth-month bees
>   hum;
> Give me faces and streets! give me these phantoms incessant and
>   endless along the trottoirs!
>
> . . . .
>
> Give me such shows! give me the streets of Manhattan!
> Give me Broadway, with the soldiers marching—give me the sound
>   of the trumpets and drums!
> (The soldiers in companies or regiments—some, starting away,
>   flush'd and reckless;

Some, their time up, returning, with thinn'd ranks—young, yet very
    old, worn, marching, noticing nothing;)
   . . . .

People, endless, streaming, with strong voices, passions, pageants;
Manhattan streets, with their powerful throbs, with the beating
    drums, as now;
The endless and noisy chorus, the rustle and clank of muskets, (even
    the sight of the wounded;)
Manhattan crowds with their turbulent musical chorus—with varied
    chorus and light of the sparkling eyes;
Manhattan faces and eyes forever for me.[50]

This is writing after the Fall, and it suggests not only the urban basis
of Whitman's vision but a change in his self-conception. The whole will
not come back again, the poet knows; "archaic" satisfactions no longer
obtain.[51] But Whitman dramatizes that recognition as the ground of
mature vision. He builds a constitutive lack into his depictions of the
city just as he builds a constitutive lack into his conception of democracy. Unlike the pastoral fields, this is a space of inadequacy and desire:
no longer full-sized, ranks are "thinn'd" and "worn"; no longer "full-
dazzling," objects flicker past in shadowy parade. The massive theatricality of Whitman's city—its "shows" and "pageants"—calls attention to
this artifice, this fall into representation. These are not real people but
book people, as Alcott might say, not the real body but figments, fabrications: "phantoms incessant and endless." Whitman willingly exchanges a
poetry of full presence for a poetry of hints and glances, "faces and eyes."
The wounded soldiers enter the poem as a consequence of that recognition, an emblem of the poet's decision to "trampl[e] down" his former
cries and confront what he "sought to escape": the partiality of body and
language, the fragility of sexual relations, the contingency of human
knowledge. But this insight does not paralyze the poet. He "revers[es]"—
but does not stifle—his cries. As Frost would say, "The question that he
frames in all but words / [i]s what to make of a diminished thing."[52] What
Whitman makes of this knowledge is the self-consciously "wounded"

poetics of the Civil War, a romance art of phantom and fragment, a convalescent art open to the incompleteness of body and vision, and able to
admit, only then, "even the sight of the wounded."

What results in *Memoranda During the War* is a mode of writing care-
fully tailored to confront the cultural ethos of postwar America. There is
little trace here of the epic ambition of the first two editions of *Leaves of
Grass*—the grand desire to give the world its "New Bible," its "Great
Construction."[53] The last thing America needed in 1875 was another
Totalitarian Construction—another "total solution" to the conflicts of
American life, another "centralization of thoughts, feelings, and views on
national subjects."[54] There was plenty of that to go around. Whitman
makes the far more innovative and politically daring decision to
"revers[e]" himself, as he puts it in "Give Me the Splendid Silent Sun,"
and reimagine the democratic premise of his writing. In self-conscious
resistance to the totalitarian spirit of the Gilded Age, Whitman reinvents
his role and writing once again, as he had done many times before.

"Unwieldy and immense, who shall hold in behemoth?" Whitman
asked in *Democratic Vistas*, "who bridle leviathan?" Who better than
Whitman himself?—a poet who had once sought to create in *Leaves of
Grass* an American leviathan, a gigantic political and poetic body absorbing all others into itself: "what I assume you shall assume." That assumption did not survive the Civil War; indeed it did not survive the homosexual indirections of "Calamus." But the democratic impulse that
produced that ambition did survive, although in a different and unexpected form. This is now lower-case art: not a "Great Construction" but
a few fragments, a handful of scraps and pieces literally scissored out and
patched together from notebooks, journalism, poem fragments, and letters. The book itself would be pulled apart and put back together in different forms at different times: as "Memoranda of a Year" (1863), "'Tis
But Ten Years Since" (1874), *Memoranda During the War* (1875), a section of *Two Rivulets* (1876), and finally as a section of *Specimen Days and
Collect* (1882). Throughout these reconstructions Whitman pursues his
most radical investigation of the relation between writing and wreckage:

the "*litter*-rary" remains, as he liked to put it, that command his attention after the war.[55] The feel of the *Memoranda* itself is loose and splintered: its vision is rapid and glancing, and its landscapes are littered with debris: corpses, refuse, leavings, ash heaps, amputations, bleached bones, tufts of hair, buttons, fragments of clothing, the remains of the hospitals, the remains of the regiments, the remains of his own comprehensive ambition—what he later called his "Notes Left Over."[56]

The leavings of the war are the counter-sign of Totalitarian Union. Remains embarrass comprehensive summary. They undermine what Whitman calls "the idea and fact of AMERICAN TOTALITY" by exposing what is left out by that totality, what remains untotaled, untallied, or unknown.[57] Under the eye of the hospital doctor, the body becomes "exhaustively legible," Foucault says, "open without remainder to the sovereign dissection of language and of the gaze."[58] Whitman recovers and cherishes that "remainder." In contrast to totalitarian forms of control, Whitman exposes what is left out by political and medical knowledge: the "leavings" of the army hospitals (p. 55), the "*escapees*" of the Confederate army (p. 4), the remains of uncounted dead. These remains—what Derrida calls *restance*, the "left-overness" of representation[59]—disable comprehensive authority. They advertise the inadequacy of totalitarian control, even the poet's own.[60]

"After you have exhausted what there is in business, politics, conviviality, love, and so on—have found that none of these finally satisfy, or permanently wear—what remains?" Whitman asks in *Specimen Days*.[61] It is the central question of his war: what is left out of artistic representation ("There is something else there"); what is left out of social history ("The real war will never get in the books"); what is left out of the conventions of death and public ceremony ("Unnamed, unknown, remain, and still remain, the bravest soldiers"). The fact that something else remains in each instance of closure reveals that closure as incomplete, an as yet unaccomplished totality that makes room for the ongoing work of medicine, poetry, and democracy.

This is the negative ambition of *Memoranda During the War,* the negative space of the gay romance. "[T]here are qualities of the American people which find no representation, no voice," the poet writes in *November Boughs.*[62] Whitman devotes his art to those qualities after the war. He offers no "complete or epical presentation" but stresses instead the inadequacy of representation to contain the real—what he calls "the real war," what Alcott calls "the genuine article."[63] In either case, it "will never get in the books" and that loss, first confronted in 1856, deeply influenced the writings that followed.

The romance tradition in American literature provided the poet with an epistemology and a politics exactly suited to his needs as both a gay and a democratic writer. What Hawthorne calls the "glimpses, sketches, and half-developed hints" of the romance make room for a latent humanness.[64] They signal realms of thought, feeling, sexuality, and experience inadequately represented by the official discourses of American culture. The romance casts doubt on claims of absolute truth and thrives on a creative uncertainty at odds with absolute power. Subverting the closure of his text, and in this sense sacrificing his ambition to write a comprehensive Civil War history, Whitman sustains that uncertainty, the gay mistrust marking his hospital work as a whole. The partial views of the *Memoranda* release the war from the strictures of its narration and hold open the prospect that authentic democracy might yet emerge from the sacrifices of the dead. In this sense the *Memoranda,* like *Specimen Days,* is a negative book—"I was quite willing to write an immensely *negative* book"[65]—one that seeks to distinguish the living uncertainties of American democracy from the deformed and deadened simulacra of the Gilded Age.

FIVE

The Art of the Suture

Richard Selzer and Medical Narrative

These hospitals—so different from all others—these thousands
and tens and twenties of thousands of American young men
badly wounded, operated on, pallid, with diarrhea, languishing,
dying, with fever, pneumonia &c open a new world somehow
to me, giving closer insights, new things, exploring deeper
mines than any yet, showing our humanity, . . . bursting the
petty bonds of art.

Walt Whitman, Notebooks

Whitman's influence on American poetry is well known and studied.
The repercussions of his art ripple out to touch poets as diverse as Hart
Crane, Allen Ginsberg, June Jordan, and Pablo Neruda. But Whitman's wild children include a sprinkling of doctors as well, writers like
Richard Maurice Bucke, William Osler, William Carlos Williams, and,
perhaps most directly, Richard Selzer. "I am a Dresser of wounds," Selzer writes in his recent story, "Pages from a Wound-Dresser's Diary,"
adopting as his own the persona of Whitman during the Civil War.[1]
Selzer is drawn to Whitman not by an interest in democratic theory,
but by his interest in a specific mode of medical narrative, one that
oscillates between closure and divergence and values that suspense as a

sign of vitality. The suspense of Selzer's writings emerges not only in the negative capability of gay healers modeled on Whitman, nor only in the uncertainty of his patients' conditions. It emerges most powerfully in Selzer's description of the doctor-writer himself, a figure, as he says, "suspended between . . . two worlds," and subject to an ongoing and creative "dissatisfaction":

> Such a life, the life of a writing doctor, is not without its own special risk. William Butler Yeats told of Fergus, a king of Ireland, who abdicated his throne in order to learn the "dreaming wisdom"— poetry. A Druid gave Fergus a little bag of dreams—"a small slate-colored thing"—to make him forget that he ever was a king. But it did not work. Poor Fergus was suspended between the two worlds, swinging from one to the other in restless dissatisfaction. Which is about where a writing doctor is apt to find himself. The two halves of his life may be as incompatible as those of Fergus. A doctor must insulate himself against the powerful impact of mortal lessons; a writer must learn to gaze upon them with fully dilated pupils. It is not an easy thing to do both at the same time.[2]

Like Whitman, Selzer proposes a way of writing the body that can live in that suspense. He responds to the dilemma of the writing doctor by exploring a narrative mode that both affirms and undermines its own coherence. What results in Selzer is a complex oscillation between two terms, "two worlds": stability and dilation, closure and drift, fact and romance. These are "the opposite negations," as Emerson would say, "between which, as walls, his being is swung."[3] This oscillation has a rich history in American literature and medicine, one that includes the therapeutic skepticism of conservative medicine, the symbolic reversals of nursing adventure stories, the duplex structure of the American romance, and the gay mistrust of mainstream science and art. This oscillation is intensely present in Whitman's depictions of sick and injured bodies, as we've seen. It is the rhythm of his romance of medicine.

Whitman was a poet with an eye on the future. He was acutely aware of the rise and fall of literary reputations, and he hated to think that his poetry might someday become quaint or irrelevant like the genteel poets he learned from and despised. He wanted, above all, to be useful to a future America, and he believed that the reader best suited to understand his project would have to be a doctor. It seems fitting, then, to conclude this study by looking closely at how one doctor has used Whitman's romance of medicine, the Civil War writings most often dismissed as "obsolete," even during the poet's lifetime.[4] Self-consciously joining his voice and text with Whitman's, Selzer carries this tradition forward. He develops the characteristic tensions of Whitman's romance—the characteristic "struggle between conflicting, paradoxical, opposing elements"[5]—but he imagines those tensions in a new way, through the figure of the *suture*. Disrupting a fictive as well as a corporeal deadening, Selzer's writings remain conflicted, inconclusive. He both desires and resists the suture's closure, and he invests his stories with an openness of possibility only partly comprehended or controlled. The homosexual erotic is a sign of that partial control, the sign of a restorative uncertainty in Selzer's writing of the body. Opening his text to that uncertainty, Selzer develops the implications of Whitman's romance in specific and powerful ways.

DRIFTING IN AND OUT

"Pages from a Wound-Dresser's Diary" is based on John Lauderdale's Civil War letters to his sister Frances (Frank) Lauderdale of Geneseo, New York. Lauderdale was a contract surgeon in the western theater of the Civil War, and his letters from that period are now held in the Beinecke Library at Yale, where Selzer read them as he was writing "Pages from a Wound-Dresser's Diary." Lauderdale's descriptions provide the historical setting for Selzer's story, and many specific episodes and images in "Pages from a Wound-Dresser's Diary" are taken directly from the Lauderdale papers. But the language and title of the story, and the persona of the wound-dresser himself, are Whitman's. "I wanted to write about the events that took place on this steamboat, and its effect on the doctor, his role," Selzer explained to Charles Schuster in 1982:

> But I also wanted to use language. And I remembered that Walt Whitman had been a wound dresser during the Civil War . . . and in fact wrote a poem called "The Wound Dresser." So. Now I had it. I had the way to get into this material. . . . I wrote it in the form of a diary, fragmented, using the language that approximates Whitman. In fact my character I describe from a photograph of Whitman as wound dresser. I use the word "wound dresser" as the title. I was making no secret of the fact that I was relying on Whitman's life experience and applying it, applying the poetry, applying the poetic sensibility to the events in this young doctor's life.[6]

The variety of tones and voices in "Pages from a Wound-Dresser's Diary"—itself a compound mixture of myth, history, fiction, and poetry—resists an easy definition. It refuses to settle easily into one genre or another, one perspective or another. And it renders explicit the narrative and erotic errancy so important to Whitman's medical writings. Selzer's story centers on a passionate desire between the older wound-dresser, named William, and a dying soldier named Elisha. The beautiful fluency of Selzer's story develops in part from a gay erotic that does not settle into fixed or normative patterns. The homosexual healer wanders in Selzer, as he does in Whitman. He works and writes in passing on his riverboat, aloof from all moorings, and afloat.

Like *Memoranda During the War,* "Pages from a Wound-Dresser's Diary" is told in pieces, in diary entries without connecting commentary. The Mississippi River itself is unbridged in this story, conspicuously "unspanned." "Say that a man is missing a finger," William remarks. "So forever after he is known as 'Fingers.' It is a peasant wisdom that invents a man from what he does not have. There is a fine accuracy to such nicknames; I call this river 'Bridges,' for it has hardly any. . . . This Mississippi unspanned is no place to be."[7]

"Fingers," "Bridges": such names do not compensate for loss, they reinscribe it. They do not mask absence but keep it fresh, keep reminding the man, in the intimacy of his own name, of "what he does not have." Language is a poor dressing at such moments. It fails—flagrantly and repeatedly in this story—to stabilize the flux of William's experience. "Up sack! You gone," the dockworkers sing, loading cargo onto the Mississippi riverboats. "Oh I whoop my woman and I black her eye / But I won't cut her th'oat kaze I skeered she might die. / Up sack! You gone."[8] The song becomes the wound-dresser's own lament, his own violent farewell, as he cuts not only the throats, but the arms, legs, and eyes of the soldiers strewn over the steamboat's deck, its freighted cargo. "A snip of the scissors, and it, too, is gone."[9] William's doctoring, like his writing, is elegiac, a lesson in loss. And there is little healing in this work, precious little "wound-dressing," as he is made to feel, like "Fingers," the irony of his own name. At times, Selzer depicts a coercive closure, a medical and literary control that constricts its subject. But in "Pages from a Wound-Dresser's Diary" he explores the opposite condition—the felt need for closure, for some way of making sense of this chaos, some way of staying for a while what is passing, rapidly, away. "You gone."

Whitman's Civil War writings record this loss as well. "I don't know how you feel about it," he confessed to his friend, Thomas Sawyer, "but it is the wish of my heart to have your friendship, and also that if you should come safe out of this war, we should come together again in some place where we could make our living, and be true comrades and never be separated while life lasts."[10] It is a wish neither wound-dresser achieves. There is no place, finally, where gay love can settle and consolidate itself in Whitman or Selzer. And the setting of Selzer's story—"the Mississippi unspanned"—is precisely appropriate to the Whitman persona, one that coincides with the "no place" of the homosexual lover: "The Mississippi unspanned is no place to be."

The wounded lover enters Selzer's story as a fourteen-year-old fifer-boy named Elisha. "He has pale yellow hair and blue eyes," William says. "I carry him from the litter to a cot, and his head falls against my chest. Suddenly I feel myself to be a comet hurtling through the sky."[11] Like Orpheus, the fifer-boy sings back to life the older man's passion and joy. But William, too, loves this young man but is immediately to lose him. "I unwrap the gauze from [Elisha's] forehead and hold him once again over the side of the boat," William writes shortly before Elisha's death. "Looking down into the Yazoo, we can see the avulsion of his brow. It cannot be stitched, so much tissue having been torn away. Elisha studies it. And as I gaze with him down into the river, I see in the water behind his head the yellow noonday sun. There is the great red star-shape on his forehead, and, behind it, the sun. For a moment, I cannot say for certain. Is it the wound that hangs in the sky and the sun that blazes between the eyes of the boy?"[12]

Elisha's wound resists comprehension. It resists "suturing," and the doctor "cannot say for certain" what the wound or the love really means. The scene is an echo not only of the wound-dresser texts but of Whitman's great river-poem, "Crossing Brooklyn Ferry." Looking into the reflected sunlight of the East River, Whitman sees his own beatific vision: "the fine centrifugal spokes of light round the shape of my head in the sunlit water."[13] The strange, almost religious, resonance of Elisha's wound recalls Whitman's image. Single figures "commingle" in this moment—rivers run together—and we cannot say for certain where one leaves off and another begins. "[F]lowing beneath these sounds the low ceaseless murmuring of three hundred men drifting in and out of private dreams," Selzer writes, "I cannot tell where their whispering leaves off and the whispering of the river begins."[14]

Such "drifting in and out" is the characteristic of Whitman's nursing, the intermingling of actual and imaginary he terms "the romance of surgery and medicine." Returning to that romance, Selzer evokes a fluid, interstitial space between youth and age, fact and dream. He proposes, moreover, a mode of narrative that is itself transitional, a commingling of voices—Lauderdale's, Whitman's, Selzer's own. As double- (or triple-) voiced discourse, "Pages from a Wound-Dresser's Diary" embraces a discursive fluency moving in and out of different styles, "drifting in and out" of different voices. The drift of river and voice undermines stable certainties: "I cannot tell," William says. "I cannot say for certain." But it makes possible a way of knowing freed from rigid perspectives and devoted to the inconclusiveness of an open-ended present. Immersing himself in the river's flow, indeed feeling himself "taken over by the river," Selzer's wound-dresser discovers in that drift the unexpected possibilities of healing and love: "I probe the putrid depths of the great sore," William explains in the story's conclusion. "The man shudders to feel me there. My finger meets the hard blunt tip of a minié ball. I fish it out and hold it up for the man to see. Very faintly, he smiles. All at once a strange feeling comes over me. It is happiness. I cannot resist it. And I know that if love came once, it may come again. If love should not come, still I know why I am alive."[15]

THE SUTURE

The river drift of voice and desire is one side of Selzer's art. Erotic and narrative uncertainty is offset, however, by a rigorous, technical competence Selzer associates with the surgeon's suture: "At first glance, it would appear that surgery and writing have little in common, but I think that is not so," Selzer writes in "The Pen and the Scalpel." "The surgeon sutures together the tissues of the body to make whole what is sick or injured; the writer sews words into sentences to fashion a new version of human experience. A surgical operation is rather like a short story. You make the incision, rummage around inside for a bit, then stitch up. It has a beginning, a middle and an end."[16]

The desire "to make whole what is sick or injured" relates the work of surgery and writing, and the surgeon's instrument of closure, the suture, emerges for Selzer as a sign of that dual concern. Literally, *sutur-*

ing is a technique of wound closure, the art of joining the split edges of the skin in a graft or seam. But suturing implies a larger issue in Selzer's writings, and he uses the suture to image textual as well as bodily acts of closure. Writing, for Selzer, can be an instrument of healing and repair, a way of closing off uncertainty and restoring a sense of continuity and shared meaning. Literary closure creates "a sense of appropriate cessation," Barbara Herrnstein Smith writes: "It announces and justifies the absence of further development; it reinforces the feeling of finality, completion, and composure which we value in all works of art; and it gives ultimate unity and coherence to the reader's experience."[17]

Whether or not we value "ultimate unity" in "all works of art," its appeal for a medical writer is unmistakable. Narrative "heals" by restoring a "disrupted connectedness," Howard Brody argues:

> The sick or anguished patient experiences himself as being in a terrifying and mysterious "middle" that seems to make no sense. The physician comforts and makes the experience understandable and controllable by supplying an account of a beginning and an end that make the "middle" comprehensible in relation to them. . . .
> . . . [R]elief of suffering comes most often by changing the meaning of the experience for the sufferer and restoring the disrupted connectedness of the sufferer with herself and those around her.[18]

Responding to the radical disordering of disease, Selzer's stories offer, at times, the assurance of restored control—a beginning, a middle, and an end. Medical narrative, like medical treatment, can impose restraint. It can resist the terrible inventiveness of affliction and return the patient to conservative, recognizably human, forms of experience. At such times, it is not the loss of the proper name but its recovery that seems to matter most. "What is your name?" a surgeon asks a Honduran girl disfigured by cleft lip and cleft palate. "Imelda," she answers, but the name is indistinguishable, inhuman: "The syllables leaked through the hole with a slosh and a whistle." The surgeon works to repair Imelda's lips. He tries to fix her voice and face and restore a connectedness disrupted by the girl's "defect." Her wound was "utterly hideous," the narrator comments, "a nude rubbery insect."[19] Medicine responds to this dehumanization, and in that response it is necessarily conservative. Its ethical imperative, Victor Kestenbaum argues, is "to 'restore the patient's humanity,' which has been 'wounded' by the diminishments and obstructions characteristic of the experience of illness."[20]

Suturing names this impulse in Selzer, the deeply felt desire to restore connectedness. But if suturing is in some way inevitable in medical narrative, Selzer remains particularly attentive to the coercive possibilities of this process, the violence implicit in this desire for closure. In a story such as "Brute," for instance, Selzer shows how the suture constricts, even mutilates, its subject, in order to restore control. In this story, a man is taken to an emergency room under police restraint. His head is lacerated and bleeding, and he seems to the physician-narrator less a human being than a wild animal: "I am ravished by the sight of him, the raw, untreated flesh." As he cleans and debrides the wound, the physician urges the man to remain still: "'Hold still,' I say. 'I cannot stitch your forehead unless you hold still.'" Looking up from the table, the man answers, "*You* fuckin' hold still," and his fight with the police now becomes a fight with a physician who is equally determined to restrain him.[21] As the patient struggles against this restraint, the violence of the physician's technique intensifies, and he sutures, finally, not the wound, but the man himself, literally sewing the man's earlobes to the mattress of the stretcher:

> I go to the cupboard and get from it two packets of heavy, braided silk suture and a large curved needle. I pass one of the heavy silk sutures through the eye of the needle. I take the needle in the jaws of a needle holder, and I pass the needle through the center of his right earlobe. Then I pass the needle through the mattress of the stretcher. And I tie the thread tightly so that his head is pulled to the right. I do exactly the same to his left earlobe, and again I tie the thread tightly so that his head is facing directly upward.

"I have sewn your ears to the stretcher," I say. "Move, and you'll rip 'em off." And leaning close I say in a whisper, "Now *you* fuckin' hold still."[22]

Such suturing is not ignored in Selzer's work. It is not excluded from an otherwise seamless and stabilizing presentation. Instead, Selzer urges the recognition of an unresolved and at times violent conflict at the heart of his writings: a desire to still the life of the patient in order to know and repair it—"you fuckin' hold still"—and an antithetical desire to disrupt that stillness, to resent it, indeed to identify it as a kind of death.

Enacted in many of Selzer's stories, this conflict evokes a broader concept in aesthetic and psychoanalytic theory, a concept also called, in both French and English, the *suture*. Based largely on the work of Jacques Lacan, the concept of the suture was introduced into psychoanalysis by Jacques Alain Miller and into film and narrative theory by Jean-Pierre Oudart, Daniel Dayan, Stephen Heath, and Kaja Silverman.[23] Although not identical in emphasis and meaning, suturing for these theorists refers to a fundamental premise: the claim that works of art expose and then cover over the inadequacies of their subject. They promote an awareness of wounding in order to relieve it, to suture it, in a way that stabilizes the viewer or reader within a preexisting social order. The more intense the threat of negation and loss, the more intense the desire for closure.[24] And it is this desire that relates the concept of the suture across several fields. Framing, point-of-view editing, perspective, subject positioning, narrative closure: these and other devices perform the function of the suture by allowing a reader or viewer to ward off the recognition of discord and stabilize a threatened coherence.

Stability, however, has its price, and suture theory emphasizes the constricting, ideologically conservative effects of the suture in narrative and in film. Creating and then satisfying a desire for closure, the sutured text binds the reader to normalizing cultural roles. "[W]e want suture so badly," Kaja Silverman explains, "that we'll take it at any price, even with the fullest knowledge of what it entails."[25] Suture theory is most convincing as it specifies this price: alternative discourses, alternative sexualities, alternative futures. The sutured text eliminates these alternatives, and it stabilizes, then, not only identity but also power. As Silverman explains:

> Suture can be understood as the process whereby the inadequacy of the subject's position is exposed in order to facilitate (i.e., create the desire for) new insertions into a cultural discourse which promises to make good that lack. Since the promised compensation involves an ever greater subordination to already existing scenarios, the viewing subject's position is a supremely passive one, a fact which is carefully concealed through cinematic sleight-of-hand.[26]

These "already existing scenarios" are the cherished, uncritical myths of social order. They are the unifying constructs of gender or class or race by which a text stabilizes itself and its readers. Rejecting that subordinating stability, what Silverman calls a "castrating coherence,"[27] suture theory deconstructs the closure of classical narrative, seeing in that closure a key instrument of control. By promoting, and then relieving, psychic and social discord, the sutured text keeps still—holds still—a resistant heterogeneity.

If suture theory finds in Lacan its model of the subject, it finds in Louis Althusser its model of power. For what most distinguishes the system of the suture is its invisibility, the fact that its operations are "carefully concealed." The classical narrative authorizes power by disguising its conflicts—its own deep cuts—and re-presenting the familiar myths of culture as coherent and inevitable. We are unable to see the suturing process itself, these theorists claim. We are unable to see meaning being made, being constructed, and we thus "absorb an ideological effect without being aware of it."[28]

Suturing, then, is the process by which narrative makes whole what is sick or injured, but this wholeness depends on what Noël Carroll calls "fictions of coherence": "[S]uture stops manifestations of absence by binding the subject into fictions of coherence." To preserve these fictions, the classical narrative masks or effaces its own artifice. "[A]ny sutured totality does not include the representation of the suturing process itself within its representation," Carroll explains. The suture "is excluded from the film."[29]

Carroll's claim marks an important difference from Selzer's work. Far from excluding the suturing effect, Selzer's stories are explicitly about it. The suture is not carefully concealed in "Brute." Its coherence is not made to seem transparent or inevitable. Closure in Selzer results from highly mediated, at times highly violent, acts of construction. This difference from suture theory stems in part from the actual medical practice out of which Selzer's writings emerge. The suture is more than a metaphor for Selzer, just as subject inadequacies are more than "gaps," more than theoretical wounds. Selzer explores the concept of the suture with a material complexity notably missing from suture theory itself. And he insists on representing aesthetic and conceptual issues in terms of the physical body. Closure, binding, absence, suturing: the core terms of suture theory gain weight in Selzer as they are thought through on the body itself, rendered visible in embodied scenes of suffering and care.

Suture theory is, however, still useful for medical narrative as it complicates a traditional understanding of closure. Where traditional narrative identifies connectedness as a moral or aesthetic imperative, suture theory rejects that imperative and identifies as its own therapeutic goal an enabling recognition of loss.[30] Where traditional narrative supports the power of writing to control meaning and to "relate individual experiences to the explanatory constructs of the society,"[31] suture theory exposes the illusion of that control and urges our interrogation of the social constructs that make it possible. Where traditional narrative welcomes final, lasting resolutions, suture theory rejects such resolution and shows how texts reinscribe an absence they cannot stop signifying. Suture theory, in short, questions uncritical affirmations of closure and calls attention to the writer's inability to suture his or her subject completely.

This inability lies at the center of Selzer's work. Selzer does not disavow the restorative effects of the suture. He is devoted to what Carroll calls "fictions of coherence," but like Whitman he is determined to preserve both terms in that conception: both the coherence of the subject *and* a recognition that this coherence is contrived. "[F]or you know," Selzer writes, "that the lovely precise world of proportion contains, just beneath, *there*, all disaster, all disorder."[32] Where traditional narrative urges us to value that proportioned world, suture theory urges us to distrust it, and to recognize the crippling effects of its purported unity. Selzer's accomplishment depends on his ability to see and move between both terms. He refuses to deconstruct narrative closure and celebrate, in the midst of horrific suffering, an anarchic heterogeneity. But he also refuses fully to subordinate the competing elements of his fiction and create a straight-line discourse cured of conflict. Without renouncing scientific and aesthetic control, Selzer complicates it—actively incompletes it—and produces an open-ended, dialogic mode of medical discourse.[33] Out of this tension, Selzer explores a way of writing the body that could both promote and relieve its strangeness, a writing that, as we've seen in Whitman, could both close and keep from closing.

This conflict is acted out on the body of Alexis St. Martin. In the eponymous story, Selzer again explores conceptual issues of closure and control in terms of the embodied, erotic relation between two men: the physician and scientist William Beaumont and his patient, a Canadian woodsman named Alexis St. Martin. St. Martin is injured by an accidental shotgun blast that opens a wound in his abdomen and exposes a portion of his stomach. Although he survives his injury, St. Martin's wound remains open for the rest of his life. In treating the wound, Beaumont begins a series of experiments on St. Martin's stomach that grows into a life-long scientific and erotic relation. Selzer emphasizes the unresolved conflict in this relation, Beaumont's conflicted desire both to close his lover's wound and to keep it from closing. Even as he seeks to cure his patient and bring his relation with St. Martin to an end, Beaumont resists that ending, works against it, and harbors, as Selzer says, a "secret hope that the wound would *not* heal." "Where lies the truth?" Selzer asks, reflecting on this relationship: "Since history fails to inform absolutely in this critical matter, one is left to one's own interpretative devices. I prefer to think of Beaumont as tortured by his conflicting desires: to keep the wound from healing, and to ensure that it healed."[34]

"Alexis St. Martin" is an embodied investigation of Selzer's own dilemma as a medical writer: his own conflicting desires both to bring his stories to an end and to keep them from ending, both to heal the deviations of his text and to keep them from healing. Beaumont stands as a figure for this conflict, an erotic, medical, and narrative discontent emerging frequently in Selzer's essays and stories. Selzer stages this discontent as a disruptive response to finalizing tendencies in his own work. Like Beaumont, Selzer both desires and resists closure and his writings enact an ongoing drama of control. "On and on they battled," Selzer writes, "Beaumont to 'procure,' 'secure,' and 'gain control of' his laboratory animal; St. Martin for his freedom from the demonic doctor who, he must never forget, had *saved his life*."[35] Unable to "complete" his experiments and "regain possession" of the "elusive St. Martin," Beaumont is not exceptional for Selzer: his is "the best known, most beloved tale in all of American medicine."[36] What is exceptional is Selzer's ability to render this conflict directly, his ability to reclaim erotic, irrational, and anti-formalist impulses within medicine and so evoke the limits of control. Medicine is not monologic for Selzer, not consistent or fully binding. It is instead disrupted, and vitalized, by conflict, by the doctor's inability to cure what Selzer calls the "petulance, the coquetry, the recalcitrance of St. Martin."[37]

By its very nature, medicine works to reform this recalcitrance. It restructures the body within stable diagnostic and therapeutic categories, tending thereby toward closure and comprehension. This stabilizing impulse is the subject of Selzer's "Letter to a Young Surgeon—II." In this reflection on art and surgery, Selzer recounts a surgeon's practice of cutting out his patients' navels during abdominal operations, literally remaking the shape of their bodies in order to achieve a more perfect closure. This surgeon's suturing expresses a desire for what Selzer calls "the continuous straight line"—a normative, "undeviate" closure far distant from the erotic conflicts of "Alexis St. Martin":

> [T]his surgeon had become annoyed by the presence of the navel, which, he decided, interrupted the pure line of his slice. Day in, day out, it must be gone around, either to the right or to the left. Soon, what was at first an annoyance became a hated impediment that must be got rid of. Mere circumvention was not enough. And so, one day, having arrived at the midpoint of his downstroke, this surgeon paused to cut out the navel with a neat ellipse of skin before continuing on down to the pubis. Such an elliptical incision when sutured at the close of the operation forms the continuous straight line without which this surgeon could not live. Once having cut out a navel . . . and seeing the simple undeviate line of his closure, he vowed never again to leave a navel behind. . . . Years later I would happen upon one of these bellies and know at once the author of the incision upon it.[38]

The surgeon is both doctor and artist, "the author of the incision," and his sutures are a kind of writing, a medical signature. But the surgeon-writer's desire for perfect closure leads him to ignore and violate the actual body of the patient. He overrides the body's impediments and replots it on a rational grid, reconstructing the patient within precise, geometric forms. This geometric reduction of the body, however, is anything but a desirable alternative to the conflicting energies of "Alexis St. Martin." There is no erotic bias in this surgeon's stroke, no deviation from "the pure line of his slice." But this sutured closure is deeply coercive—a mutilation, Silverman's "castrating coherence"—and Selzer rejects its "simple undeviate line" as a satisfying medical and narrative end.

The reductive geometry of lines and grids emerges often in Selzer's depictions of surgery. "It is simply a matter of dropping the upper lip into a normal position, then crossing the gap with two triangular flaps," another surgeon explains in "Imelda," describing how to repair the child's cleft lip. "It is geometry."[39] The "gaps" of the child's face in "Imelda," like the "impediments" of the patient's body in "Letter to a Young Surgeon—II," are repaired by the surgeon's sutures. They are closed, fixed—"I will fix your lip"—and this fixing is a gesture of conceptual as well as technical control.[40] "Marking pen!" the surgeon commands in preparing Imelda for surgery. "He placed the first blue dot at the apex of the bow. The nasal sills were dotted; next, the inferior philtral dimple, the vermilion line. The *A* flap and *B* flap were outlined. On he worked, peppering the lip and nose, making sense out of chaos, realizing the lip that lay waiting in that deep essential pink, that only he could see."[41] Again like an artist, Praxiteles realizing a buried form, the surgeon plots a Cartesian grid over the child's face, remaking her wound into a coherent, symmetrical shape: an equilateral triangle. The girl is literally written upon in this surgery, marked by a vermilion "Λ" in a way that confirms the surgeon-writer's mastery: his ability to make sense of her face, to suture her difference, to sign her with a scarlet letter. But if this signing is imaginatively or psychologically deadening for Hawthorne, it is literally deadening in "Imelda." The girl dies during her operation. The straight lines of the surgical tracing are ironically and fatally duplicated in the flat line of her EKG monitor, and Selzer identifies the coherence of "the continuous straight line" as a sign of death, a sign of the end. "'He's going to die,'" Selzer writes of a surgical patient in "Sarcophagus." "'The minute I take away my pressure, he'll bleed to death.' I try to think of possibilities, alternatives. I cannot; there are none."[42] As in "Imelda," the loss of interpretive possibility presages the patient's death in this story: "The line droops, flattens. The man is dead."[43]

Compelled to resist this deadening, this flat-line closure, Selzer occupies a conflicted, indeed paradoxical, position as a medical writer. Like the surgeon in "Letter to a Young Surgeon—II," Selzer longs for the undeviate closure of a fully settled, fully comprehended meaning. "Everything here . . . is touched by a golden light that is uncontaminated, healing," Selzer writes in the dream vision of "Amazons." "It is a light in which there can be no misunderstanding."[44] But this dream of full closure—of clefts perfectly joined, of meaning fully conveyed—is death-like, a termination. And Selzer responds to this recognition by obstructing the closural impulse in his own narrative: contaminating his prose with multiple, conflicting possibilities, and calling our attention to the vitality of the unstilled body.

Selzer's paradoxical desire both to achieve and to undermine narrative closure is not unique. The novel itself is divided between conflicting impulses, Bakhtin argues, an "impulse to continue" and an "impulse to end."[45] This conflict is constitutive of the novel for Bakhtin, as also for Jonathan Culler and D. A. Miller. Flaubert's narratives "resist recuperation while at the same time inviting it," Culler argues, a paradox suggestive of what Culler calls "a pathology of the novel."[46] Similarly, D. A. Miller points out the "curiously perverse" project of writers such as Austen, Eliot, and Stendhal who both desire and draw back from a "definitive, 'finalizing' state of affairs. . . . Their narratives stubbornly reach after what, as narratives, they seem intrinsically prevented from being. Accordingly, each novelist raises a problem far more radical than the specific problems furnished by the actual narrative: the problem of there being a narrative at all."[47] What emerges in Bakhtin, Culler, and Miller as a general property of narrative, however, is specifically related to the dilemma of the writing doctor for Selzer, a writer torn between an impulse to close or cure the anomaly of his subject, and a contrary impulse to sustain that anomaly as a sign of ongoing vitality. But what looks "perverse" to Miller or "pathological" to Culler—scientifically and textually deviate—is importantly therapeutic in the larger context of Selzer's work, an alternative to an undeviate, and death-like, line of closure.

After her death, Imelda's surgeon completes his operation, fixing the face of a now dead girl. And Selzer describes the child's "repair" in a passage that could have been written by Poe:

> He is ready to suture. He fits the tiny curved needle into the jaws of
> the needle holder. Each suture is placed precisely the same number

of millimeters from the cut edge, and the same distance apart. He
ties each knot down until the edges are apposed. Not too tightly.
These are the most meticulous sutures of his life. He cuts each
thread close to the knot. It goes well. The vermilion border with its
white skin roll is exactly aligned. One more stitch and the Cupid's
bow appears as if by magic. . . .

   . . . Where the cleft had been there was now a fresh line of tiny
sutures.[48]

The girl's face is "aligned," finally, delicately beautiful, but it is the
beauty of the corpse, a suturing on the face of the dead.

   Against this stilled beauty, Selzer's patients mark themselves, even
wound themselves, in gestures of independence and self-will. In "Raccoon," for example, a patient cuts open her own freshly sutured abdomen with a razor blade, and reaches into her body in an uncanny imitation of the surgeon himself:

> The woman is naked. She sits on the toilet, bent forward, her pale
> white feet floating on the jammy floor. Nearby, a razor blade
> dropped from one painted hand. The other hand cannot be seen; it
> is sunk to the wrist within the incision in her abdomen. Bits of black
> silk, still knotted, bestrew the floor about her feet. They are like the
> corpses of slain insects. The elbow which points out from her body
> moves in answer to those hidden fingers which are working . . .
> working.[49]

The scene is bizarre and terrifying, and Selzer's title suggests his inability to bring it under control, to give it a human name or context. The
torn sutures in "Raccoon"—the "[b]its of black silk"—image this failure,
the doctor-writer's inability to close off and make sense of what he calls
the "mystery" of the woman's wound. This mystery is profoundly unsettling to the doctor, profoundly resonant and alive. And it calls attention
to a deadening implicit in the suture itself. It is not the wound but now
the suture that seems inhuman, a dead insect: "They are like the corpses
of slain insects."

Like his sutures, the doctor's discourse is conservative, neutralizing. It attempts to minimize the damage and recompose both patient and surgeon against the opening of the act itself. "It's all right," he says. "Don't worry. We'll fix it. You didn't realize."[50] But it is precisely the doctor's and the writer's inability to "fix" this mystery that Selzer's story evokes, and in its closing lines it is not the patient but now the surgeon who is discomposed, opened: "'When you are calm,' I say, 'we'll go back to the operating room, and I will stitch you up again.' 'I *am* calm,' she says. 'You are the one who isn't calm.'"[51] Selzer's stories work against this calm. They do not end in repose and quiescence. They do not recover an equilibrium disrupted but now restored. Instead, Selzer exposes the insufficiency of narrative and medical treatments in the face of what cannot be fully settled, what cannot be easily or finally *stitched up*. As Eric Cassell observes:

> In illness . . . we attempt to understand, but the disease process is beyond our control and the significance of events is often beyond our knowledge. Because in this instance lack of understanding threatens our completeness and exposes us to unknown dangers, we make new and repeated interpretations with added emotional content to compensate for a deficient reality. Rather than bringing comfort, each new interpretation only shows more clearly the tattered edges of our understanding.[52]

Selzer exposes these "tattered edges," these "[b]its of black silk." Like the patient in "Raccoon," his stories reopen themselves, reinscribing an incompleteness they seem, on the one hand, to heal, to suture. The wounded body "burst[s] the petty bonds of Art," Selzer writes, quoting from Whitman's Civil War notebooks,[53] a bursting made literal in the broken sutures of "Raccoon." The wounded body exposes the reductiveness of its treatment, the "petty bonds" of medical and literary representation. It thus provokes new and repeated efforts to represent affliction more fully, to comprehend it within more flexible and appropriate frames of mind. But these renewed efforts will themselves fall short, remain partial, and expose, yet again, "the tattered edges of our understanding." We have no assurance at the end of "Raccoon" that this second operation will be successful—"we'll go back . . . and I will stitch you up again." We have no assurance that this second treatment will finally cure the woman's mystery, that *these sutures* will finally hold. But rather than conceal this effect, Selzer is determined to expose it, to call attention to it as both the dilemma and the opportunity of his art. And in this gesture we sense his debt to Whitman.

In 1863 Whitman met Lewy Brown, a Maryland soldier wounded at Rappahannock Station and brought to Armory Square Hospital in Washington. Whitman was present during the amputation of Brown's leg and described the operation in his notebook:

> To-day, after dinner, Lewy Brown had his left leg amputated five
> inches below the knee. . . . I was present at the operation, most of
> the time in the door. . . . Lewy came out of the influence of the
> ether. It bled & they thought an artery had opened. They were to
> cut the stiches again & make a search but after some time concluded
> it was only surface bleeding. They then stitched it up again & Lew
> felt every one of these stiches, though yet partially under the influ-
> ence of ether. . . . I could hear his cries sometimes quite loud, & half
> coherent talk & cought glimpses of him through the open door. At
> length they finished, & they brought the boy in on his cot, & took it
> to its place. I sat down by him. . . . As usual in such cases he could
> feel the lost foot & leg very plainly. The toes would get twisted, &
> not possible to disentangle them.[54]

Whitman could not bring himself to publish this scene, except in pieces: the inward suffering of the nurse-witness reoccurs in "The Dresser"; the glimpse through the open door shapes the angle of vision in the *Memoranda*; the eerie presence of the lost limb reappears in the "phantoms" of "Give Me the Splendid Silent Sun"; even Brown's "half coherent talk" returns in the dying voice of Jonathan Wallace. Whitman will treat this scene many times in his hospital and Civil War writings. He will go back, like the surgeons themselves, and "stitch it up again," knowing full well that these sutures, too, will not hold. This is the difficult truth of Whitman's romance of medicine. As a writer and nurse, Whitman affirms the need to name and control affliction, to stabilize the experience of suffering and suture a deeply felt sense of loss. But he also affirms the value of what evades and disturbs that control, the value of what cannot be fully treated, sutured, comprehended, or closed off. It is, in the end, that uncertainty—the suspense of an unsettled, uncomprehended subject—that Whitman and Selzer cherish in their writings as a sign of vitality, and an alternative, then, to the stillness of the sutured dead.

NOTES

INTRODUCTION

1. Nathaniel Hawthorne, *The House of the Seven Gables: A Romance* (New York: New American Library, 1961), p. 190.

2. Walt Whitman, *Walt Whitman: The Correspondence*, vol. 1, ed. Edwin Haviland Miller (New York: New York University Press, 1961), pp. 68–69.

3. Nathaniel Hawthorne, *The Scarlet Letter*, in *Great Short Works of Nathaniel Hawthorne*, ed. Frederick C. Crews (New York: Harper and Row, 1967), p. 33.

4. Walt Whitman, *November Boughs*, in *Walt Whitman: Complete Poetry and Collected Prose*, ed. Justin Kaplan (New York: Literary Classics of the United States, 1982), p. 1214.

5. "It is immense, the best thing of all, nourishes me of all men," Whitman wrote of his war experience in 1863. See Whitman, *Correspondence* 1: 82. This passage also appears in *Notebooks and Unpublished Prose Manuscripts*, vol. 2, ed. Edward F. Grier (New York: New York University Press, 1984), p. 595.

6. Whitman, *Correspondence*, 1: 163.

7. Walt Whitman, *The Uncollected Poetry and Prose of Walt Whitman*, vol. 2, ed. Emory Holloway (Garden City, N.Y.: Doubleday, Page, 1921), p. 91.

8. Walt Whitman, *Walt Whitman: The Correspondence*, vol. 2, ed. Edwin Haviland Miller (New York: New York University Press, 1961), p. 86.

9. Whitman, *Notebooks*, 2: 591.

10. Abraham Lincoln, *The Collected Works of Abraham Lincoln*, vol. 2, ed. Roy P. Basler (New Brunswick, N.J.: Rutgers University Press, 1953), p. 405. Lincoln adds that he is "horrified at the thought of the mixing blood by the white and black races" (p. 407) and urges a "separation of the races [as] the only perfect preventive of amalgamation" (p. 408). Lincoln's "horror" is shared by many. On the fear of miscegenation as a political force in American culture, see Kenneth M. Stampp, *The Peculiar Institution: Slavery in the Ante-Bellum South* (New York: Alfred A. Knopf, 1956), pp. 350–61; and Joel Williamson, *New People: Miscegenation and Mulattoes in the United States* (New York: Free Press, 1980). On Whitman's own fears of race amalgamation, see *I Sit and Look Out: Editorials from the Brooklyn Daily Times* (New York: Columbia University Press, 1932), p. 90. For a discussion of Lincoln's attitudes toward race, see Eric J. Sundquist, *Faulkner: The House Divided* (Baltimore: Johns Hopkins University Press, 1983), pp. 96–130; and *To Wake the Nations: Race in the Making of American Literature* (Cambridge: The Belknap Press of Harvard University Press, 1993), pp. 79, 131–34.

11. On the male purity movement, see G. J. Barker-Benfield, *The Horrors of the Half-Known Life: Male Attitudes toward Women and Sexuality in Nineteenth-Century America* (New York: Harper and Row, 1976), pp. 135–74; and Michael Moon, *Disseminating Whitman: Revision and Corporeality in "Leaves of Grass"* (Cambridge: Harvard University Press, 1991), pp. 19–25.

12. Carroll Smith-Rosenberg, *Disorderly Conduct: Visions of Gender in Victorian America* (New York: Alfred A. Knopf, 1985), p. 261.

13. Lincoln, *Collected Works*, 2: 461.

14. Robert Penn Warren, *The Legacy of the Civil War: Meditations on the Centennial* (New York: Random House, 1961), pp. 22–23.

15. Lincoln, *Collected Works*, 3: 550. On the movement in American political thought toward a concept of absolute Union, see Paul C. Nagel, *One Nation Indivisible: The Union in American Thought, 1776–1861* (New York: Oxford University Press, 1964). On the absolutist tendency in Whitman's own concept of Union, see Timothy Sweet, *Traces of War: Poetry, Photography, and the Crisis of the Union* (Baltimore: Johns Hopkins University Press, 1990), pp. 11–78.

16. Lincoln, *Collected Works*, 2: 461.

17. Walt Whitman, *Leaves of Grass (1891–92)*, in *Walt Whitman: Complete Poetry and Collected Prose*, ed. Justin Kaplan (New York: Literary Classics of the United States, 1982), p. 565.

18. Quoted in Allen Grossman, "The Poetics of Union in Whitman and Lincoln: An Inquiry toward the Relationship of Art and Policy," in *The American Renaissance Reconsidered: Selected Papers from the English Institute, 1982–83,* eds. Walter Benn Michaels and Donald E. Pease (Baltimore: Johns Hopkins University Press, 1985), p. 187. In this influential essay, Grossman contrasts Lincoln's and Whitman's concepts of Union. "Unlike Lincoln's God," Grossman writes, "who cannot be for and against the same thing at the same time, Whitman's 'greatest poet' inferred from the traditional fame-powers of his art a fundamental principle of undifferentiated representation, which constituted a massive trope of inclusion" (p. 187).

19. Walt Whitman, *Walt Whitman's "Memoranda During the War" and Death of Abraham Lincoln,* ed. Roy P. Basler (Bloomington: Indiana University Press, 1962), p. 65.

20. Whitman, *Leaves of Grass (1891–92),* p. 233. "The sign and credentials of the poet are, that he announces that which no man foretold," Emerson writes in "The Poet." "He is the true and only doctor." Ralph Waldo Emerson, *Essays and Lectures,* ed. Joel Porte (New York: Literary Classics of the United States, 1983), p. 450. Jerome Loving singles out this essay as "the Emersonian fountainhead of Whitman's poetry." See "Emerson, Whitman, and the Paradox of Self-Reliance" in *Critical Essays on Walt Whitman,* ed. James Woodress (Boston: G. K. Hall, 1983), p. 306.

21. George B. Forgie, *Patricide in the House Divided: A Psychological Interpretation of Lincoln and His Age* (New York: W. W. Norton, 1979), p. 159.

22. Whitman, *Correspondence,* 1: 69.

23. Oliver Sacks, *A Leg to Stand On* (New York: Harper and Row, 1984), p. 164. I am indebted to Sacks's powerful reflections, in this work and others, on convalescence, Nietzsche, and the suspense of the afflicted body.

24. My argument draws on several studies emphasizing poetic and political mediation in Whitman. "Claiming to reconcile racially distinct bodies, Whitman locates the poet in the sexually charged middle space between masters and slaves," Karen Sánchez-Eppler argues. As "the common place" between self and other (Donald E. Pease), the "neutral territory" between known and unknown (William Aarnes), "the expressive site and medium" between the many and the one (Kerry Larson), "the conjunctive term" between the general and particular (Allen Grossman), the "liminal landscape" between rigid social structures (George B. Hutchinson), the "liminal space" between rigid sexual identities

(Michael Moon), or the "liminal place" between life and death (James Dougherty)—Whitman's "charged middle space" takes many forms. In each case, Whitman's conception of the poet as mediator suspends a static opposition and stands between exclusive or contradictory terms. See Karen Sánchez-Eppler, *Touching Liberty: Abolition, Feminism, and the Politics of the Body* (Berkeley: University of California Press, 1993), p. 50; Donald E. Pease, "Blake, Crane, Whitman, and Modernism: A Poetics of Pure Possibility," *PMLA* 96 (1981), p. 76; William Aarnes, "'Almost Discover': The Spiritual Significance of Soldier Talk in Whitman's *Specimen Days*," *Walt Whitman Review* 28 (1982), pp. 88–89; Kerry C. Larson, *Whitman's Drama of Consensus* (Chicago: University of Chicago Press, 1988), p. xvi; Allen Grossman, "The Poetics of Union," p. 201; George B. Hutchinson, *The Ecstatic Whitman: Literary Shamanism and the Crisis of the Union* (Columbus: Ohio State University Press, 1986), p. xxiv; Moon, *Disseminating Whitman*, p. 11; and James Dougherty, *Walt Whitman and the Citizen's Eye* (Baton Rouge: Louisiana State University Press, 1993), p. 87.

25. David Cavitch, *My Soul and I: The Inner Life of Walt Whitman* (Boston: Beacon Press, 1985), p. 44. Cavitch's emphasis on Whitman's creative decline and political withdrawal after 1860 is shared by many. See, for example, Edwin Haviland Miller, *Walt Whitman's Poetry: A Psychological Journey* (Boston: Houghton Mifflin, 1968), pp. 10–18, 208–24; Stephen A. Black, *Whitman's Journeys into Chaos: A Psychoanalytic Study of the Poetic Process* (Princeton: Princeton University Press, 1975), pp. 221–33; C. Carroll Hollis, *Language and Style in "Leaves of Grass"* (Baton Rouge: Louisiana State University Press, 1983), pp. 88–123; Paul Zweig, *Walt Whitman: The Making of the Poet* (New York: Basic Books, 1984), p. 343; Larson, *Whitman's Drama of Consensus*, pp. 207–44; M. Jimmie Killingsworth, *Whitman's Poetry of the Body: Sexuality, Politics, and the Text* (Chapel Hill: University of North Carolina Press, 1989), pp. 131–54; Tenney Nathanson, *Whitman's Presence: Body, Voice, and Writing in "Leaves of Grass"* (New York: New York University Press, 1992), pp. 477–97; and Dougherty, *Walt Whitman and the Citizen's Eye*, pp. xvi, 108–35.

There are, however, several dissenting voices. In a book as campy and loose as Whitman himself, Charley Shively shows how Whitman's democracy and homosexuality were in fact confirmed by the community of gay lovers he discovered in the Civil War hospitals. I rely heavily on Shively's account of Whitman's hospital culture. With a different tone and approach, Betsy Erkkila disputes conventional claims that Whitman depoliticized his work after 1860 and argues instead for the continuing vitality of Whitman's vision of democracy and homosexuality after the war. My debt to Erkkila, however, runs deeper. Erkkila's *Whitman the Political Poet* introduced into Whitman scholarship an expanded concept of the "political." Erkkila attends to Whitman's explicit political interests, but she also explores what she calls "the more subtle and less conscious ways his poems engage on the level of language, symbol, and myth the particular power struggles of his time" (p. v). It is this general method, more perhaps than her specific readings, that has influenced my study. Michael Moon also complicates a restricted notion of Whitman's canon by showing how the fourth (1867) edition of *Leaves of Grass* is actually "closer to the body" than any other group of Whitman poems. It is thus possible to read Whitman's Civil War writings, Moon suggests, "as a direct continuation and extension of the male-homoerotic political project inaugurated in 'Calamus'" (p. 211). That claim is central to my study as well. See Charley Shively, *Drum Beats: Walt Whitman's Civil War Boy Lovers* (San Francisco: Gay Sunshine Press, 1989); Betsy Erkkila, *Whitman the Political Poet* (New York: Oxford University Press, 1989); Betsy Erkkila, review of *Whitman's Poetry of the Body: Sexuality, Politics, and the Text*, by M. Jimmie Killingsworth, *Walt Whitman Quarterly Review* 7, no. 4 (1990), pp. 194–97; Betsy Erkkila, "Whitman and the Homosexual Republic," in *Walt Whitman: The Centennial Essays*, ed. Ed Folsom (Iowa City: University of Iowa Press, 1994), pp. 153–71; and Moon, *Disseminating Whitman*, pp. 171–222.

26. "I have thought a sort of Itinerary of my Hospital experience might be worth while from a Democratic point of view & even be specially serviceable," Whitman wrote in a manuscript note. Charles Glicksberg, ed., *Walt Whitman and the Civil War: A Collection of Original Articles and Manuscripts* (Philadelphia: University of Pennsylvania Press, 1933; reprint, New York: A. S. Barnes, 1963), p. 166.

27. Here and at several other places in my argument—chapter 1, in particular—I draw on two essays by Mitchell Robert Breitwieser, one on Whitman and one on Jefferson. Breitwieser's emphasis in both essays is on the provisionality of democratic representation. The totality of the popular will is never wholly coincident with its figures of authority, Breitwieser argues, never wholly caught or realized by its own representation. In Whitman, this idea leads to the poet's creation of a general or universal voice, a transcendent "I" untrapped by the local manifestations of its appearance. In Jefferson, this tension results from the focal disparity between theory and experience in Jefferson's landscape writing,

but it culminates once again in a specifically political vision: "a form of government in which an awareness of the provisionality of political representation—its discrepancy from the population it aims to represent—would be structurally central" ("Jefferson's Prospect," pp. 325–26). This discrepancy is central to Whitman's view of democratic representation, I argue, but unlike Breitwieser I see that discrepancy emerging not from attempts to map a landscape or record a voice but from Whitman's attention to the physical body. See Mitchell Robert Breitwieser, "Who Speaks in Whitman's Poems?" in *The American Renaissance: New Dimensions*, ed. Harry R. Garvin (Lewisburg, Penn.: Bucknell University Press, 1983), pp. 121–43; and "Jefferson's Prospect," *Prospects* 10 (1985), pp. 315–52.

28. See Moon, *Disseminating Whitman*, pp. 1–25; and Erkkila, "Whitman and the Homosexual Republic," pp. 156–58.

29. My summary of heroic medicine is based on John Harley Warner, *The Therapeutic Perspective: Medical Practice, Knowledge, and Identity in America, 1820–1885* (Cambridge: Harvard University Press, 1986); Richard Harrison Shryock, *Medicine and Society in America, 1660–1860* (New York: New York University Press, 1960); John S. Haller, Jr., *American Medicine in Transition, 1840–1910* (Urbana: University of Illinois Press, 1981); Martin S. Pernick, *A Calculus of Suffering: Pain, Professionalism, and Anesthesia in Nineteenth-Century America* (New York: Columbia University Press, 1985); and Stewart Brooks, *Civil War Medicine* (Springfield, Ill.: Charles C. Thomas, 1966).

30. Warner, *Therapeutic Perspective*, p. 40.

31. Henry Burnell Shafer, *The American Medical Profession, 1783–1850*, Faculty of Political Science of Columbia University, eds., Studies in History, Economics and Public Law, No. 417 (New York: Columbia University Press, 1936), p. 97, quoted in Martha Banta, "Medical Therapies and the Body Politic," *Prospects* 8 (1983), p. 87.

32. T. G. Thomas, *Introductory Address Delivered at the College of Physicians and Surgeons, New York, October 17th, 1864* (New York: Trafton, 1864), p. 31, quoted in Charles E. Rosenberg, *The Care of Strangers: The Rise of America's Hospital System* (New York: Basic Books, Inc., 1987), p. 87.

33. The obstetrician John King recommended this procedure to control childbed convulsions. See Pernick, *Calculus of Suffering*, p. 45.

34. Quoted in Harold Aspiz, *Walt Whitman and the Body Beautiful* (Urbana: University of Illinois Press, 1980), p. 42.

35. Warner, *The Therapeutic Perspective*, p. 41.

36. James Jackson, Jr., to James Jackson Sr., Paris, 24 November 1832, quoted in Warner, *The Therapeutic Perspective*, p. 26.

37. Emily Miller Budick, *Engendering Romance: Women Writers and the Hawthorne Tradition, 1850–1990* (New Haven: Yale University Press, 1994), p. 4. Budick also traces the skepticist implications of the romance in *Fiction and Historical Consciousness: The American Romance Tradition* (New Haven: Yale University Press, 1989), pp. ix–xiii, 119–63.

38. "M. Louis on Typhoid Fever," *Western Lancet* 1 (1842–43), p. 375, quoted in Warner, *The Therapeutic Perspective*, p. 201.

39. Budick, *Engendering Romance*, p. 5.

40. Warner, *The Therapeutic Perspective*, p. 41.

41. Whitman, *Memoranda During the War*, p. 3.

42. Whitman, *Notebooks*, 2: 484.

43. D. A. Miller, *Narrative and Its Discontents: Problems of Closure in the Traditional Novel* (Princeton: Princeton University Press, 1981), p. ix.

44. Largely implicit in Whitman, this theory of medical narrative emerges most directly in the twentieth century medical writer Richard Selzer, as I argue in chapter 5.

45. George B. McKnight, "Notes Taken on Lectures Given by David Hosack on the Theory and Practice of Physic and Clinical Medicine, New York, 1814–16," Joseph M. Toner Papers, quoted in Warner, *The Therapeutic Perspective*, pp. 46–47.

46. Ralph Waldo Emerson, "Self-Reliance," in *Essays and Lectures*, ed. Joel Porte (New York: Literary Classics of the United States, 1983), p. 265

47. Glicksberg, ed., *Walt Whitman and the Civil War*, p. 24.

48. See Thomas L. Brasher, *Whitman as Editor of the Brooklyn "Daily Eagle"* (Detroit: Wayne State University Press, 1970), p. 184; and Aspiz, *Walt Whitman and the Body Beautiful*, pp. 37–75.

49. On the history of a homosexual "sensibility," see Michel Foucault, *The History of Sexuality*, vol. 1: *An Introduction*, trans. Robert Hurley (New York: Random House, 1978), p. 43; and Byrne R. S. Fone, *Masculine Landscapes: Walt Whitman and the Homoerotic Text* (Carbondale: Southern Illinois University Press, 1992), pp. 17–19, 30. Fone provides a useful summary of the debates surrounding this concept as well as a brief history of the homosexual response to Whitman (pp. 272–76 nn. 21 and 23).

50. Quoted in Oscar Cargill, introduction to *The Wound Dresser*, by Walt Whitman (New York: The Bodley Press, 1949), p. vii.

51. Amanda Akin Stearns, *The Lady Nurse of Ward E* (New York: Baker and Taylor, 1909), p. 57.

52. *The Letters of John Keats*, ed. Maurice Buxton Forman (New York: Oxford University Press, 1935), p. 72. According to Justin Kaplan, Whitman underlined this passage in his copy of Keats. See *Walt Whitman: A Life* (New York: Simon and Schuster, 1980), pp. 189–90. For a discussion of Keats's definition of poetic identity as it relates to Whitman, see Kenneth M. Price, *Whitman and Tradition: The Poet in His Century* (New Haven: Yale University Press, 1990), pp. 18–21. For a discussion of negative capability as a linking term in literature and medicine, see G. S. Rousseau, "Literature and Medicine: Towards a Simultaneity of Theory and Practice," *Literature and Medicine* 5 (1986), p. 159; and Charles I. Schuster, "The Nonfictional Prose of Richard Selzer: An Aesthetic Analysis," in *Literary Nonfiction: Theory, Criticism, Pedagogy*, ed. Chris Anderson (Carbondale: Southern Illinois University Press, 1989), p. 10.

53. Moon, *Disseminating Whitman*, p. 176.

54. Whitman, *Leaves of Grass (1891–92)*, p. 285.

55. For a counter-argument, see Nathanson, *Whitman's Presence*, pp. 406–43. Nathanson argues, by way of Lacan, that homosexual circulation in "Calamus" mimes a heterosexual economy of exchange and so perpetuates the structures it appears to subvert.

56. Walt Whitman, *Democratic Vistas*, in *Walt Whitman: Complete Poetry and Collected Prose*, ed. Justin Kaplan (New York: Literary Classics of the United States, 1982), p. 982. I intend to take Whitman at his word in this passage and explore the convergence between sexuality and politics in this period of his career. I thus see my work building on a number of critics who read Whitman's democratic theory through the homosexual body. Such writers include Robert K. Martin, *The Homosexual Tradition in American Poetry* (Austin: University of Texas Press, 1979); Joseph Cady, "Not Happy in the Capitol: Homosexuality and the Calamus Poems," *American Studies* 19, no. 2 (fall 1978), pp. 5–22; Joseph Cady, "*Drum-Taps* and Nineteenth-Century Male Homosexual Literature," in *Walt Whitman: Here and Now*, ed. Joann P. Krieg (Westport, Conn.: Greenwood Press, 1985), pp. 49–59; Killingsworth, *Whitman's Poetry of the Body*; Erkkila, *Whitman the Political Poet*; and "Whitman and the Homosexual Republic"; Shively, *Drum Beats*; Moon, *Disseminating Whitman*; and Christopher Newfield,

"Democracy and Male Homoeroticism," *The Yale Journal of Criticism* 6, no. 2 (1993), pp. 29–62.

Of these critics, only Shively and (to some extent) Erkkila see Whitman's Civil War writings, as I do, as the culmination of his vision of democracy as the "twin or counterpart" of gay love. Shively's account of that culmination, however, is restricted to Whitman's biography and private correspondence. Erkkila affirms the inseparability of democracy and homosexuality in Whitman's Civil War writings but construes the basis of that convergence differently, as I discuss in chapter 1. I am indebted to Martin's general claim that Whitman's poetry is historically important not because it depicts this or that homoerotic act but because it helps to fashion a distinct homosexual consciousness. Cady also sees Whitman's Civil War poetry as a self-conscious "homosexual affirmation" ("Male Homosexual Literature," p. 50), but he does not pursue the democratic implications of gay love. In fact, Cady critiques Whitman's appeal to democracy in the "Calamus" poems as a "lapse" in the homosexual vision of the collection ("Not Happy in the Capitol," pp. 11–12). Both Killingsworth and Moon describe a sharp division between the radical body politics of the early *Leaves of Grass* and what Killingsworth calls the "depoliticized" poetry written after 1860 (p. 136). Moon's Lacanian reading of Whitman's Civil War poetry explores a thematics of phallic domination. Although Moon's study is one of the most nuanced investigations to date of the sexual politics of Whitman's work, his reading of the fourth (1867) edition of *Leaves of Grass* reduces that work to the narrow dimensions of a psychological drama, and, like Killingsworth, Moon concludes that the democratic and homoerotic project of *Leaves of Grass* did not survive the war (p. 221). Newfield does not include Whitman's Civil War writings in an argument that stresses the subversive potential of gay love to defeat competitive hierarchies.

Although I've drawn on Byrne R. S. Fone's analysis of Whitman's gay sensibility, and learned from his close readings, Fone is not particularly interested in the political consequences of Whitman's homosexuality. Indeed Fone's disturbing celebration of homosexual rape as a "sacramental" act suggests, if anything, a politics of domination quite different from the democratic ethos I discover in Whitman's Civil War writings. See Fone, *Masculine Landscapes*, pp. 68–89.

57. Walt Whitman, *Specimen Days*, in *Walt Whitman: Complete Poetry and Collected Prose*, ed. Justin Kaplan (New York: Literary Classics of the United States, 1982), p. 768. Paul Zweig discusses this tension in *Walt Whitman*, pp. 339–43.

58. Whitman, *Correspondence*, 1: 187.

59. Christopher Flint, "Flesh of the Poet: Representations of the Body in *Romancero gitano* and *Poeta en Nueva York*," *Papers on Language and Literature* 24, no. 2 (spring 1988), p. 198.

60. Friedrich Nietzsche, *The Gay Science*, trans. Walter Kaufmann (New York: Vintage Books, 1974), p. 35. *The Gay Science* begins with an epigraph from Emerson's "History," and the title itself may be an allusion to what Emerson called the "Joyous Science" in his 1876 lecture "The Scholar." Walter Kaufmann discusses Emerson's influence on Nietzsche in his "Translator's Introduction," pp. 7–13. See also George J. Stack, *Nietzsche and Emerson: An Elective Affinity* (Athens: Ohio University Press, 1992).

61. Nietzsche, *The Gay Science*, p. 34.

62. Ibid., p. 36.

63. Ralph Waldo Emerson, "Intellect," in *Essays and Lectures*, ed. Joel Porte (New York: Literary Classics of the United States, 1983), p. 426.

64. Nietzsche, *The Gay Science*, p. 32.

65. Ibid., p. 35.

66. Barbara Spackman, "Nietzsche, D'Annunzio, and the Scene of Convalescence," *Stanford Italian Review* 6, nos. 1–2 (1986), p. 152.

67. Kaufmann, "Translator's Introduction," p. 5.

68. Walter Kaufmann, *Nietzsche: Philosopher, Psychologist, Antichrist* (Princeton: Princeton University Press, 1974), p. 34 n. 10. In *Whitman and Nietzsche*, C. N. Stavrou makes a similar claim, arguing that the "peculiar intensity of emphasis many pretend to discover in the staunch advocacy of male friends in Whitman and Nietzsche can be shown—where it is not an undigested gob of pruriency in the pretenders—to be entirely logical and quite normal." In some of the most flamboyantly homophobic language I've ever read in academic discourse, Stavrou pronounces his anathema on readers who interpret male friendship in Whitman and Nietzsche as homoerotic: "Scabrous succubi, *soi-disant* literary analysts, have, like insolent Catilines, abused our patience long enough. When they tell us Whitman's celebration of the friend is anything more or anything less than a protest against the cruelty, hypocrisy, deceit, and callousness inhering in the relations between man and his fellow, they speak less than truth." See *Whitman and Nietzsche: A Comparative Study of Their Thought* (Chapel Hill: The University of North Carolina Press, 1964), pp. 165, 167–68.

Emphasizing Nietzsche's influence on what she calls the "male-erotic-centered anarchist tradition" of European philosophy, Eve Kosofsky Sedgwick discovers in Nietzsche "an open, Whitmanlike seductiveness, some of the loveliest there is, about the joining of men with men, but [Nietzsche] does so in the stubborn, perhaps even studied absence of any explicit generalizations, celebrations, analyses, reifications of these bonds as specifically same-sex ones." *Epistemology of the Closet* (Berkeley: University of California Press, 1990), p. 133.

69. Whitman, *Specimen Days*, p. 780. Nietzsche also presents himself as a lifelong convalescent in his autobiography, *Ecce Homo*, and he assumes the persona of "Der Genesende" in *Thus Spake Zarathustra*. On this, see Spackman, "The Scene of Convalescence," p. 150. Whitman's enthusiastic response in 1849 to F. Wüldmuller's painting "Convalescence" suggests an early example of the poet's interest in this idea. See Joseph Jay Rubin, *The Historic Whitman* (University Park: Pennsylvania State University Press, 1973), p. 239.

70. The central importance of the convalescent body in Whitman's postwar writings complicates some traditional accounts of Whitman's career. Harold Aspiz, for example, claims that Whitman largely abandoned the body in his writings after 1860. Whitman's "postwar writings stress the spiritual and ethical elements of human experience rather than the physical ones," Aspiz claims. Whitman's political essays draw "little sustenance from [his] physical biography" (*Walt Whitman and the Body Beautiful*, pp. 95, 5). Whitman's emphasis on the convalescent body signals a major shift in his work, a turn from what Aspiz calls the "physically superb prophet-teacher" of the early *Leaves of Grass* (p. 6). Whitman is clearly a different poet after 1860, but just as clearly he is a poet who continues to affirm the centrality of the physical body—now wounded and infirm—to his understanding of democratic politics and art. Before the war, Whitman sought to ground democratic identity on the self-evident certainty of the healthy body. The "physically superb prophet-teacher" tropes the intense vigor and fertility of the American nation and provides a unifying ground of national consensus. That consensus and that appeal give way by 1860 and what emerges in its place is Whitman's emphasis on the suspense of the afflicted body. The implication of that shift—from health to disease, from self-evidence to uncertainty, from the fullness of bodily life to the "partial recovery" of convalescence—is a major concern of my study.

71. Whitman, *Specimen Days*, p. 736.

72. Ibid., p. 718.

73. Walt Whitman, "The Eighteenth Presidency!" in *Walt Whitman:*

Complete Poetry and Collected Prose, ed. Justin Kaplan (New York: Literary Classics of the United States, 1982), p. 1310.

74. Budick, *Engendering Romance*, p. 5.

75. Whitman, *Democratic Vistas*, p. 929. Whitman echoes this formulation in his discussion of "the subtle vitalization and antiseptic play call'd Health in the physiologic structure." See *November Boughs*, p. 1243.

76. Friedrich Nietzsche, *Beyond Good and Evil: Prelude to a Philosophy of the Future*, trans. Walter Kaufmann (New York: Vintage Books, 1966), p. 90.

CHAPTER ONE

1. Walt Whitman, *Democratic Vistas*, in *Walt Whitman: Complete Poetry and Collected Prose*, ed. Justin Kaplan (New York: Literary Classics of the United States, 1982), p. 946.

2. George M. Fredrickson, *The Inner Civil War: Northern Intellectuals and the Crisis of the Union* (New York: Harper and Row, 1965), pp. 65–78, 98–112. See also Gregory Eiselein's discussion of "coercive humanitarianism" in nineteenth-century discourses of consolation and mourning. Eiselein terms Whitman's response to those discourses, "alterative humanitarianism," a fluid, improvisational perspective open to multiple meanings and needs. I share Eiselein's emphasis on the open-ended quality of Whitman's sympathy, as I argue in chapter 3, but I see that sympathy as an expression of democratic and homoerotic elements slighted in Eiselein's discussion. See "Whitman and the Humanitarian Possibilities of 'Lilacs,'" *Prospects* 18 (1993), pp. 51–79.

3. David S. Reynolds notes the appeal of this idea to Whitman himself. See *Walt Whitman's America: A Cultural Biography* (New York: Alfred A. Knopf, 1995), p. 416.

4. On the failure of representative figures to comprehend the body politic, see Mitchell Robert Breitwieser, "Who Speaks in Whitman's Poems?" in *The American Renaissance: New Dimensions*, ed. Harry R. Garvin (Lewisburg, Penn.: Bucknell University Press, 1983), pp. 121–43; and "Jefferson's Prospect," *Prospects* 10 (1985), pp. 315–52.

5. Walt Whitman, *Walt Whitman's "Memoranda During the War" and Death of Abraham Lincoln*, ed. Roy P. Basler (Bloomington: Indiana University Press, 1962), p. 3.

6. Sharon Cameron's discussion of exemplification in Thoreau's *Journal* raises a similar set of issues. See *Writing Nature: Henry Thoreau's "Journal"* (Chicago: University of Chicago Press, 1985), pp. 3–26 and 108–54.

7. Whitman, *Memoranda During the War*, pp. 4–5.

8. On body and body politic analogies in Whitman, see Betsy Erkkila, *Whitman the Political Poet* (New York: Oxford University Press, 1989), pp. 92–128; Timothy Sweet, *Traces of War: Poetry, Photography, and the Crisis of the Union* (Baltimore: Johns Hopkins University Press, 1990), pp. 11–24; and Harold Aspiz, "The Body Politic in *Democratic Vistas*," in *Walt Whitman: The Centennial Essays*, ed. Ed Folsom (Iowa City: The University of Iowa Press, 1994), pp. 105–19. For a broader study of body politic analogies, see F. W. Coker, "Organismic Theories of the State: Nineteenth-Century Interpretations of the State as Organism or as Person," *Columbia University Studies in History, Economics, and Public Law* 38, no. 2 (1910), pp. 1–209; D. C. Phillips, "Organicism in the Late Nineteenth and Early Twentieth Centuries," *Journal of the History of Ideas* 31 (1970), pp. 413–32; Martha Banta, "Medical Therapies and the Body Politic," *Prospects* 8 (1983), pp. 59–128; and Karen Sánchez-Eppler, *Touching Liberty: Abolition, Feminism, and the Politics of the Body* (Berkeley: University of California Press, 1993), pp. 1–13.

I find Sánchez-Eppler's account of body politic arguments in antebellum America especially useful for Whitman. Drawing on and revising Carole Pateman's *The Sexual Contract* (Stanford: Stanford University Press, 1988), Sánchez-Eppler argues that the constitutional subject of the founding fathers was disembodied and fleshless, a depersonalized abstraction masking the privilege of white male power. Abolitionism and feminism unmask that privilege and substitute the racial and sexual distinctness of actual bodies—slaves, women—as a more adequate emblem of the State. Whitman likewise disputes the fiction of a disembodied State, but his understanding of social contracts depends on his experience as a gay lover and nurse. In considering feminist and abolitionist arguments, Sánchez-Eppler splits the "unitary person" of constitutional law "into a more disparate and unstable array of pieces" (p. 143 n. 3). But she does not include the homosexual body in that array, a body crucial, as we'll see, to Whitman's body politic. I thus find Sánchez-Eppler's account persuasive but partial, as she says of Pateman herself.

9. Coker, *Organismic Theories of the State*, pp. 73, 84–90.

10. George B. Forgie, *Patricide in the House Divided: A Psychological Interpretation of Lincoln and His Age* (New York: W. W. Norton, 1979), p. 98.

11. John William Draper, *Thoughts on the Future Civil Policy of America* (New York: Harper and Brothers, 1865), p. 60, quoted in Aspiz, "The Body Politic in *Democratic Vistas*," p. 107.

12. Whitman, *Democratic Vistas*, p. 966.

13. I follow Charley Shively in stressing this optimistic strain in Whitman's Civil War writings. Long after the war, Whitman remained haunted by the failure of America's democratic experiment, what he called "the lack of a common skeleton, knitting all close." But Whitman also discovered sexual and political promise in that lack, and he faced the uncertainty of a deferred or conflicted Union with much greater hope than is usually recognized. I thus present a view of Whitman quite different from the grimly defeated homosexual of Paul Zweig and M. Jimmie Killingsworth or the grimly defeated democrat of M. Wynn Thomas and Kerry C. Larson. In a striking conflation of these themes, Larson describes Whitman's Civil War writings not only as the "final defeat" of his vision of democracy but also as its "grim perversion" (p. 213). Paul Zweig, *Walt Whitman: The Making of the Poet* (New York: Basic Books, 1984), pp. 342–46; M. Jimmie Killingsworth, *Whitman's Poetry of the Body: Sexuality, Politics, and the Text* (Chapel Hill: University of North Carolina Press, 1989), pp. 136–54; Kerry C. Larson, *Whitman's Drama of Consensus* (Chicago: University of Chicago Press, 1988), pp. 207–44; M. Wynn Thomas, *The Lunar Light of Whitman's Poetry* (Cambridge: Harvard University Press, 1987), pp. 2–3.

14. Walt Whitman, *Walt Whitman: The Correspondence*, vol. 1, Edwin Haviland Miller, ed. (New York: New York University Press, 1961), p. 68.

15. Joel Porte, *The Romance in America: Studies in Cooper, Poe, Hawthorne, Melville, and James* (Middletown, Conn.: Wesleyan University Press, 1969), p. 67. Michael T. Gilmore, *American Romanticism and the Marketplace* (Chicago: University of Chicago Press, 1985), p. 84. Michael Davitt Bell, *The Development of American Romance: The Sacrifice of Relation* (Chicago: University of Chicago Press, 1980), p. 129. On Whitman's use of the romance tradition, see Richard Chase, "'Out of the Cradle' as a Romance," in *The Presence of Walt Whitman*, ed. R. W. B. Lewis (New York: Columbia University Press, 1962), pp. 52–71.

16. Porte, *Romance in America*, p. 97; Richard Chase, *The American Novel and Its Tradition* (Baltimore: Johns Hopkins University Press, 1957), p. ix; Nina Baym, *The Shape of Hawthorne's Career* (Ithaca: Cornell University Press, 1976),

p. 154. This summary is drawn in part from Lora Romero's "The Government of the Body in the American Novel, 1799–1852" (Ph.D. diss., University of California, Berkeley, 1989), pp. 212–15.

17. Whitman, *Memoranda During the War*, pp. 5–6.

18. Daniel Aaron, *The Unwritten War: American Writers and the Civil War* (New York: Alfred A. Knopf, 1973; reprint, Madison: University of Wisconsin Press, 1987), p. 268.

19. Edmund Wilson, *Patriotic Gore: Studies in the Literature of the American Civil War* (New York: Oxford University Press, 1962), p. 641.

20. Sweet, *Traces of War*, pp. 66, 5.

21. Baym, *The Shape of Hawthorne's Career*, p. 154.

22. Walt Whitman, *Specimen Days*, in *Walt Whitman: Complete Poetry and Collected Prose*, ed. Justin Kaplan (New York: Literary Classics of the United States, 1982), pp. 733–34.

23. The "unreckoned" Lincoln is a standard theme in twentieth-century Lincoln biographies, works that include *The Hidden Lincoln* (1938), *The Lincoln Nobody Knows* (1958), *The Public and the Private Lincoln* (1979), and *Abraham Lincoln, the Man Behind the Myths* (1984). On this, see Charley Shively, *Drum Beats: Walt Whitman's Civil War Boy Lovers* (San Francisco: Gay Sunshine Press, 1989), pp. 71–72.

24. The "something else" of Whitman's text echoes a key issue in Derrida's *Glas*. "The rare force of the text is that you cannot catch it," Derrida writes, "(and therefore limit it to) saying; *this is that*, or, what comes down to the same thing, this has a relation of apophantic or apocalyptic unveiling, a determinable semiotic or rhetorical relation with that, this is the subject, this is not the subject, this is the same, this is the other, this text here, this corpus here. There is always some question of yet something else." *Glas*, trans. John P. Leavey, Jr., and Richard Rand (Lincoln: University of Nebraska Press, 1986), pp. 198 (right column) and 199 (right column).

The question of "yet something else" for Derrida—the question of "what, after all, of the remain(s)" (p. 1 [left column])—emerges often in Whitman's Civil War writings, but it is related to the political ambition of his work. The rare force of democracy, Whitman might say, is that you cannot catch it, cannot limit it to any single instance of its presence. As in Lincoln, there is always some remainder, always "some question of yet something else." But this question strengthens the liberal subject for Whitman. It confirms a democratic humanism urgently at issue in the Civil War hospitals, but meaningless, or at best irrelevant, for Derrida.

25. Whitman, *Democratic Vistas*, p. 960.

26. Henry Nash Smith, *Democracy and the Novel: Popular Resistance to Classic American Writers* (New York: Oxford University Press, 1978), p. 30.

27. Whitman, *Democratic Vistas*, p. 970.

28. Donald E. Pease stresses the prospective implications of this view of democracy in *Visionary Compacts: American Renaissance Writings in Cultural Context* (Madison: University of Wisconsin Press, 1987), pp. 108–57. According to Pease, "Whitman takes such a moment—when what one is gives way to what one can be—and defines it as the ever-present and endlessly developing moment of American democracy" (p. 157).

29. Sánchez-Eppler, *Touching Liberty*, pp. 5–6.

30. Evan Carton, *The Rhetoric of American Romance: Dialectic and Identity in Emerson, Dickinson, Poe, and Hawthorne* (Baltimore: Johns Hopkins University Press, 1985), p. 3.

31. For a counter-argument, see Larson, *Whitman's Drama of Consensus*, pp. 207–44. During the Civil War, Larson claims, "[q]uestions concerning democracy's 'proof,' value, and final validation no longer engage [Whitman's] attention" (p. 216).

32. Whitman, *Specimen Days*, pp. 708–9.

33. Claude Lefort, *Democracy and Political Theory*, trans. David Macey (Minneapolis: University of Minnesota Press, 1988), p. 17.

34. Ibid.

35. Ibid., p. 16.

36. Ibid., p. 17.

37. Larzer Ziff makes this argument in "Poet of Death: Whitman and Democracy" in *Literary Democracy: The Declaration of Cultural Independence in America* (New York: Viking, 1981), pp. 244–59.

38. Whitman, *Correspondence*, 1: 69.

39. See Charles I. Glicksberg, ed., *Walt Whitman and the Civil War: A Collection of Original Articles and Manuscripts* (Philadelphia: University of Pennsylvania Press, 1933; reprint, New York: A. S. Barnes, 1963), pp. 24–47.

40. Glicksberg, ed., *Walt Whitman and the Civil War,* p. 24.

41. See Emily Miller Budick, *Engendering Romance: Women Writers and the Hawthorne Tradition, 1850–1990* (New Haven: Yale University Press, 1994), pp.

13–74. Although I am indebted to Budick's work on the epistemology of the romance, her analysis becomes less persuasive when she turns to homosexual models of desire. Because it does not end in children, such desire is barren and solipsistic, Budick claims, reproducing endless versions of itself: "Homosexuality seems to have served a purpose for Melville similar to that of incest in Faulkner's fiction: it approximated sexual intercourse with and of the self" (p. 68). For an earlier version of the "sterile" homosexual argument in reference to Whitman, see Clark Griffith, "Sex and Death: The Significance of Whitman's *Calamus* Themes," *Philological Quarterly* 39, no. 1 (Jan. 1960), pp. 18, 23, 26, 37. See also Joseph Cady's response to this argument in "Not Happy in the Capitol: Homosexuality and the Calamus Poems," *American Studies* 19, no. 2 (fall 1978), p. 14.

42. Nathaniel Hawthorne, *The Scarlet Letter,* in *Great Short Works of Nathaniel Hawthorne*, ed. Frederick C. Crews (New York: Harper and Row, 1967), p. 84.

43. By contrast, George Hutchinson argues that Whitman responded to the crisis of the Union by appropriating the founding fathers. See *The Ecstatic Whitman: Literary Shamanism and the Crisis of the Union* (Columbus: Ohio State University Press, 1986), p. 5.

44. *The Collected Works of Abraham Lincoln*, vol. 7, ed. Roy P. Basler (New Brunswick: Rutgers University Press, 1953), p. 528, quoted in Forgie, *Patricide in the House Divided*, p. 285. For filiopietistic appeals from both sides of the Civil War, see ibid., p. 285 n. 3.

45. Hawthorne, *The Scarlet Letter,* p. 93.

46. Breitwieser relates this decline in general representativeness to Whitman's political situation before the war. See "Who Speaks in Whitman's Poems?" p. 140.

47. In surveying the letters written to Whitman by his Civil War friends and lovers, Charley Shively discusses the difficulty these soldiers had in finding "the right name" for their relationship with Whitman. The interpretative problems thematized in the romance emerge powerfully in this correspondence. See *Drum Beats*, p. 54.

48. Anon. [Rufus W. Griswold], *New York Criterion* 10 November 1855; cited in Milton Hindus, ed. *Walt Whitman: The Critical Heritage* (London: Routledge and Kegan Paul, 1971), p. 33. Byrne R. S. Fone discusses the legal history of this formulation in *Masculine Landscapes: Walt Whitman and the Homoerotic Text* (Carbondale: Southern Illinois University Press, 1992), pp. 14–15.

49. Whitman, *Memoranda During the War,* p. 56.

50. "Buggery, or Sodomy," *Laws of England* (London, 1644), quoted in Christopher Newfield, "Democracy and Male Homoeroticism," *The Yale Journal of Criticism* 6, no. 2 (1993), p. 32.

51. Walt Whitman, Preface (1876), in *Walt Whitman: Complete Poetry and Collected Prose,* ed. Justin Kaplan (New York: Literary Classics of the United States, 1982), p. 1011.

52. Barbara A. Babcock, introduction to *The Reversible World: Symbolic Inversion in Art and Society* (Ithaca: Cornell University Press, 1978), p. 32. For a similar claim, see Robert K. Martin, "Whitman and the Politics of Identity," in *Walt Whitman: The Centennial Essays,* ed. Ed Folsom (Iowa City: University of Iowa Press, 1994), p. 177.

53. Friedrich Nietzsche, *Beyond Good and Evil: Prelude to a Philosophy of the Future,* trans. Walter Kaufmann (New York: Vintage Books, 1966), p. 90.

54. Jon Rosenblatt, "Whitman's Body, Whitman's Language," in *Walt Whitman: Here and Now,* ed. Joann P. Krieg (Westport, Conn.: Greenwood Press, 1985), pp. 105–6.

55. Sweet, *Traces of War,* p. 39.

56. On self-evidence in Whitman, see John T. Irwin, *American Hieroglyphics: The Symbol of the Egyptian Hieroglyphics in the American Renaissance* (New Haven: Yale University Press, 1980; reprint, Baltimore: Johns Hopkins University Press, 1983), pp. 94–98; Pease, *Visionary Compacts,* pp. 108–57; and Larson, *Whitman's Drama of Consensus,* pp. 83–93. Pease, in particular, identifies the "self-evident" as the ground of democratic consensus before the war: "Whitman believed national dissension originated when the founding principles lost self-evidence," Pease argues. "For Whitman all need for opposition, whether that of rebels against tyrants, or that of persons with opposing views, disappeared with the self-evident principles of our founding" (pp. 115, 146). What disappears by 1861 is the possibility of this appeal, and Whitman's Civil War writings affirm the "need for opposition" as a constitutive political characteristic.

57. See Cady, "Not Happy in the Capitol," pp. 6–9. In the discussion that follows I am indebted to Cady's excellent essay, although my argument differs from his in at least one respect. Like Stephen Black and Paul Zweig, Cady sees Whitman's appeals to democracy as a way of blunting or balancing the subversive potential of gay love. Unlike homosexuality, democracy is respectable and stabilizing, Cady argues, a way of returning the gay poet to the conventional

standards of a middle-class audience (p. 12). Similarly, Tenney Nathanson reads Whitman's political claims as part of "a protective distancing of more intimate, less easily acknowledged material" and thus as a retreat from the uncanny energies of the poet's exceptional presence. *Whitman's Presence: Body, Voice, and Writing in "Leaves of Grass"* (New York: New York University Press, 1992), p. 21. I discover a far more radical vision of democracy in Whitman's postwar writings, and I present that democracy not as a retreat from gay love but as its homology and culmination.

58. Walt Whitman, *An American Primer*, ed. Horace Traubel (Boston: Small, Maynard, 1904), p. 21. Betsy Erkkila singles out this passage to demonstrate Whitman's motive in using the discourses of radical democracy—comradeship, brotherhood, equality, social union—to express gay love. See "Whitman and the Homosexual Republic," in *Walt Whitman: The Centennial Essays*, ed. Ed Folsom (Iowa City: University of Iowa Press, 1994), p. 155.

59. Whitman, *Democratic Vistas*, p. 963.

60. Killingsworth, *Whitman's Poetry of the Body*, p. 132.

61. Erkkila, "Whitman and the Homosexual Republic," pp. 162–63. Erkkila complicates this convention by stressing "the inseparability of the private discourses of male homosexual desire from the more public discourses of combat and democratic nationalism" ("Whitman and the Homosexual Republic," p. 170 n. 18). I see this convergence somewhat differently. Rather than eliminating any trace of secret or private depth, Whitman's Civil War writings emphasize that quality as the shared characteristic of democracy and homosexuality. It is the sense of unrealized plenitude—the sense of "deep things, unreckoned"—that sustains the homology between democracy and homosexuality in Whitman's postwar work and suggests the proximity of these discourses to the romance.

62. See, for example, Richard Chase, *Walt Whitman Reconsidered* (London: Victor Gollancz, 1955), p. 149.

63. Whitman, *Democratic Vistas*, p. 959.

64. See Cady, "Not Happy in the Capitol," p. 8.

65. This is what Kenneth Burke calls the "promissory principle" of *Democratic Vistas*. Drawing on Burke, Alan Trachtenberg also describes Whitman's "visionary politics" as an attempt to believe in a future different from the present scene. See Kenneth Burke, "Policy Made Personal: Whitman's Verse and Prose—Salient Traits," in *"Leaves of Grass": One Hundred Years After*, ed. Milton

Hindus (Stanford: Stanford University Press, 1955), p. 76; and Alan Trachtenberg, "Whitman's Visionary Politics," *Mickle Street Review* 10 (1988), p. 24.

66. Cady, "Not Happy in the Capitol," pp. 20–21.

67. Quoted in Thomas Froncek, ed., *The City of Washington: An Illustrated History* (New York: Alfred A. Knopf, 1985), p. 219. In "Chanting the Square Deific" Whitman goes so far as to apotheosize that skepticism as a figure of the Godhead, as James Dougherty points out in *Walt Whitman and the Citizen's Eye* (Baton Rouge: Louisiana State University Press, 1993). "'Chanting the Square Deific' identifies this skeptic voice as that of Satan," Dougherty writes, "not the malignant one of *Paradise Lost* but the Satan of Job, of Blake's Milton, and of Byron—a spiritual power for dissent, self-criticism, and rebellion against constraint, here apotheosized as the fourth person of the Godhead. . . . Ever and again in *Drum-Taps*, Satan speaks forth as the voice of subversion, the accents of one who will never be absorbed by America's citizens" (p. 81).

68. "By the war's end," Paul Zweig writes, Whitman "had retreated from the vitality of his ten-year experiment. For the war was not only an ending, but a beginning: it was the beginning of his old age; the beginning of his public legend, and his stiffened, defensive stance as the 'good grey [sic] poet,' a subtly pious bard who stood for wholesome religious feeling and progress." Oscar Cargill and Harold Aspiz offer variations on the "pious bard" portrait. In a startling and—as far as I can tell—unironic comparison, Cargill believes that "*The Wound Dresser* should be held in as sacred regard as is *The Little Flowers* of Saint Francis of Assisi." For Aspiz, "the image of the Christ-like healer and the persona of Walt Whitman the hospital attendant converge into a composite and timeless figure." Zweig, *Walt Whitman*, p. 343; Oscar Cargill, introduction to *The Wound Dresser*, by Walt Whitman (New York: The Bodley Press, 1949), p. xviii; and Harold Aspiz, *Walt Whitman and the Body Beautiful* (Urbana: University of Illinois Press, 1980), p. 93.

69. Robert K. Martin, "Whitman's 'Song of Myself': Homosexual Dream and Vision," *Partisan Review* 42, no. 1 (1975), p. 83; Cady, "Not Happy in the Capitol," p. 21.

70. For a discussion of democratic skepticism that intersects with my argument here, see George Kateb, "Thinking about Human Extinction (II): Emerson and Whitman," *Raritan* 6, no. 3 (winter 1987), pp. 14–15. In a brief but valuable response to Kateb, Nancy Rosenblum disputes the assumption that democratic skepticism inclines to political tolerance, liberalism, or restraint. See

"Strange Attractors: How Individualists Connect to Form Democratic Unity," *Political Theory* 18, no. 4 (November 1990), pp. 576–85. See also David Bromwich, "Whitman and Memory: A Response to Kateb," *Political Theory* 18, no. 4 (November 1990), pp. 572–75.

71. Whitman, *Specimen Days*, p. 735; *Democratic Vistas*, p. 966.

72. Quoted in John Harley Warner, *The Therapeutic Perspective: Medical Practice, Knowledge, and Identity in America, 1820–1885* (Cambridge: Harvard University Press, 1986), p. 26.

73. Walt Whitman, *Leaves of Grass: Comprehensive Reader's Edition*, ed. Harold W. Blodgett and Sculley Bradley (New York: New York University Press, 1965), pp. 115, 123.

74. Walter Lowenfels, ed. *Walt Whitman's Civil War* (New York: Alfred A. Knopf, 1961; reprint, New York: Da Capo Press, 1989), p. 15.

CHAPTER TWO

1. Sharon Olds, "Nurse Whitman," in *Satan Says* (Pittsburgh: University of Pittsburgh Press, 1980), p. 13.

2. Andrew Delbanco discusses the relation between child-bearing and conception in Lincoln's Gettysburg Address and notes Lincoln's interest in the figure of the "nursing father." See *The Puritan Ordeal* (Cambridge: Harvard University Press, 1989), pp. 253–55, 296 n. 2.

3. I am drawing on V. V. Ivanov's analysis of mediation in "The Significance of Bakhtin's Ideas on Sign, Utterance and Dialogue for Modern Semiotics," in *Papers on Poetics and Semiotics* 4 (1976), p. 35, quoted in Peter Stallybrass and Allon White, *The Politics and Poetics of Transgression* (Ithaca: Cornell University Press, 1986), pp. 16–17. I am also indebted to Kerry C. Larson's discussion of mediation in *Whitman's Drama of Consensus* (Chicago: University of Chicago Press, 1988). Larson shows how Whitman constructs a consensual framework in the early *Leaves of Grass* in which the poem gathers without diminishment or subordination the "opposite equals" of self and other, the many and the one. Larson identifies "an ongoing dynamic of vacillation" (p. xxi) in Whitman's writings in which pairs of opposites are shown to be simultaneously present in any given work—conservative anarchism in "The Eighteenth Presidency!" intimate anonymity in "Crossing Brooklyn Ferry," tyrannical democracy in "A Song of the Rolling Earth," and validated self-evidence in "Song of

Myself." I find this vacillation particularly intense in *Drum-Taps*. I have also drawn on George B. Hutchinson's discussion of liminality in *The Ecstatic Whitman: Literary Shamanism and the Crisis of the Union* (Columbus: Ohio State University Press, 1986). In relating Whitman to the ecstatic rituals of shamanism, Hutchinson is especially interested in those moments when the "boundaries between different forms of existence, typically guarded by established codes, break down as the antistructural experience overcomes the structural" (p. xxiii). It is one instance of that breakdown, in the codes governing Civil War nursing, that I consider here.

4. Walt Whitman, *Walt Whitman: The Correspondence*, vol. 1, ed. Edwin Haviland Miller (New York: New York University Press, 1961), p. 171.

5. *Hospital Sketches* was one of the earliest and most popular accounts of Civil War nursing. Alcott conceived the narrative as a series of letters home from the Union Hotel Hospital in Georgetown, and it was first published in four issues of the *Commonwealth* from May 22 to June 26, 1863, and then republished by James Redpath later that year. Whitman read *Hospital Sketches* sometime during the summer or early fall of 1863. I am using the edition of *Hospital Sketches* in *Alternative Alcott*, ed. Elaine Showalter (New Brunswick, N.J.: Rutgers University Press, 1988), pp. 3–73. Subsequent references to *Hospital Sketches* in this chapter are cited in the text by page number.

6. David S. Reynolds provides a powerful demonstration of this claim in *Beneath the American Renaissance: The Subversive Imagination in the Age of Emerson and Melville* (Cambridge: Harvard University Press, 1988), pp. 103–12, 309–33, 507–23. In what follows, I am indebted not only to Reynolds's work on the cultural contexts of Whitman's writings but also to his discussion of symbolic mobility in the nineteenth-century literature of misery (pp. 387–437), a literature produced by writers like Alice Cary, Lillie Devereux Blake, Sara Willis Parton, Louisa May Alcott, Rebecca Harding Davis, Harriet Prescott Spofford, and Elizabeth Stoddard. Describing the mercurial transformations of Parton's sketch collection, *Fern Leaves* (1853), for example, Reynolds notes that "[f]or the first time in American literature, a woman writer showed that conventional appearances could be donned and shed like changeable masks" (p. 403). This changeability—in tone, persona, attitude, and perspective—freed women writers from confining social conventions and expressed a subversive and potentially liberating female creativity. I find this argument especially compelling for the nursing literature of the Civil War.

7. Preface (1855), in *Walt Whitman: Complete Poetry and Collected Prose*, ed. Justin Kaplan (New York: Literary Classics of the United States, 1982), p. 23.

8. See Katharine Prescott Wormeley, *The Other Side of War with the Army of the Potomac* (Boston: Ticknor, 1889); S. Emma E. Edmonds, *Nurse and Spy in the Union Army: The Adventures and Experiences of a Woman in Hospitals, Camps, and Battle-Fields* (Hartford, Conn.: W. S. Williams, 1865), also published as *The Female Spy of the Union Army* and *Nurse and Spy: or Unsexed, the Female Soldier*; Adelaide W. Smith, *Independent Volunteer: Reminiscences of an Army Nurse during the Civil War* (New York: Greaves, 1911); Jane Stuart Woolsey, *Hospital Days* (New York: D. Van Nostrand, 1870); and Fannie Oslin Jackson: *On Both Sides of the Line*, ed. Joan F. Curran and Rudena K. Mallory (Baltimore: Gateway Press, 1989).

9. For an excellent historical and biographical introduction to Alcott's nursing, see Bessie Z. Jones, introduction to *Hospital Sketches* (Cambridge: Harvard University Press, 1960), pp. vii–xliv.

10. Susan M. Reverby, *Ordered to Care: The Dilemma of American Nursing, 1850–1945* (Cambridge: Cambridge University Press, 1987), p. 43.

11. John D. Thompson and Grace Goldin, *The Hospital: A Social and Architectural History* (New Haven: Yale University Press, 1975), p. 118, quoted in Charles E. Rosenberg, *The Care of Strangers: The Rise of America's Hospital System* (New York: Basic Books, 1987), p. 128. Many American military hospitals, including Chimborazo Hospital in Richmond and Armory Square Hospital in Washington, the site of much of Whitman's work, were constructed on Nightingale's pavilion plan.

12. Cecil Woodham-Smith, *Florence Nightingale* (London: Constable, 1950), p. 348, quoted in Reverby, *Ordered to Care*, p. 43.

13. Florence Nightingale, *Notes on Nursing: What It Is, and What It Is Not* (London: Harrison, n.d.), pp. 28–29.

14. Ibid., p. 28.

15. Ibid., p. 27.

16. Ibid., p. 15. For Nightingale's influence on American nursing and medicine, see Rosenberg, *Care of Strangers*, pp. 122–41, 214–26; and Reverby, *Ordered to Care*, pp. 39–59.

17. See Rosenberg, *Care of Strangers*, pp. 23–24, 31, 292.

18. Ibid., pp. 131–32.

19. Quoted in Reverby, *Ordered to Care*, p. 44.

20. For a discussion of male and female cross-dressing in the Union army, see Charley Shively, *Drum Beats: Walt Whitman's Civil War Boy Lovers* (San Francisco: Gay Sunshine Press, 1989), pp. 17, 22, 33–40.

21. Agatha Young, *The Women and the Crisis: Women of the North in the Civil War* (New York: McDowell, Obolensky, 1959), pp. 96–97.

22. Wormeley, *The Other Side of War*, p. 126.

23. For biographical information about Edmonds, see Penny Colman, *Spies! Women in the Civil War* (Cincinnati: Betterway Books, 1992), pp. 74–76, 82; and Richard Hall, *Patriots in Disguise: Women Warriors of the Civil War* (New York: Paragon House, 1993). Charley Shively mentions Edmonds (Seelye) in his discussion of female cross-dressing (*Drum Beats*, p. 34).

24. Edmonds, *Nurse and Spy*, p. 6.

25. Valentine Mott Francis, *A Thesis on Hospital Hygiene* (New York: J. F. Trow, 1859), p. 194, quoted in Rosenberg, *The Care of Strangers*, p. 119.

26. On the concept of separate spheres in American domestic culture, see Catherine Clinton, *The Other Civil War: American Women in the Nineteenth Century* (New York: Hill and Wang, 1984); Nancy F. Cott, *The Bonds of Womanhood: "Woman's Sphere" in New England, 1780–1835* (New Haven: Yale University Press, 1977); and Ann Douglas Wood, "The War Within a War: Women Nurses in the Union Army," *Civil War History* 18 (September 1972), pp. 197–212.

27. Edmonds, *Nurse and Spy*, pp. 294–95.

28. Ibid., p. 106.

29. Ibid., p. 120.

30. According to Reverby, "Nightingale accepted as 'natural' a sexual division of labor based on biological characteristics used to justify the employment of women in occupations close to their domestic labors." *Ordered to Care*, pp. 41–42.

31. Edmonds, *Nurse and Spy*, p. 58.

32. Ibid., p. 192.

33. See, for example, Agatha Young's response to *Nurse and Spy:* "One of these female soldiers, Sarah Emma Edmonds (alias Franklin Thompson) wrote a book of reminiscences, but her adventures as she relates them are not believable and it seems clear that her story is of more interest to the clinician than to the historian." *The Women and the Crisis*, p. 104 n. 5.

34. This issue anticipates the process by which knowledge and sexuality became conceptually linked in late-nineteenth-century thought, a process Fou-

cault explores in *The History of Sexuality*, vol. 1: *An Introduction*, trans. Robert Hurley (New York: Random House, 1978). See also Eve Kosofsky Sedgwick, *Epistemology of the Closet* (Berkeley: University of California Press, 1990), p. 73; and Byrne R. S. Fone, *Masculine Landscapes: Walt Whitman and the Homoerotic Text* (Carbondale: Southern Illinois University Press, 1992), p. 269 n. 16.

35. Edmonds, *Nurse and Spy*, pp. 271–72.

36. Ibid., p. 237.

37. Walt Whitman, *Drum-Taps (1865) and Sequel to Drum-Taps (1865–66): A Facsimile Reproduction*, ed. F. DeWolfe Miller (Gainesville, Fla.: Scholars' Facsimiles and Reprints, 1959), p. 48. Subsequent references to *Drum-Taps* are from this edition and will be cited in the text by page number.

38. George M. Fredrickson, *The Inner Civil War: Northern Intellectuals and the Crisis of the Union* (New York: Harper, 1965), p. 167.

39. M. M. Bakhtin, *The Dialogic Imagination: Four Essays*, ed. Michael Holquist, trans. Caryl Emerson and Michael Holquist (Austin: University of Texas Press, 1981), p. 37.

40. Thomas Johnson, ed., *The Letters of Emily Dickinson*, vol. 2 (Cambridge: The Belknap Press of Harvard University Press, 1965), pp. 404–5, quoted in Sandra M. Gilbert, "The American Sexual Poetics of Walt Whitman and Emily Dickinson," in *Reconstructing American Literary History*, ed. Sacvan Bercovitch (Cambridge: Harvard University Press, 1986), p. 139.

41. Bakhtin, *The Dialogic Imagination*, p. 37.

42. Quoted in Showalter, introduction to *Alternative Alcott*, p. xx.

43. Louisa May Alcott, "My Contraband," in *Alternative Alcott*, p. 74.

44. Barbara A. Babcock, introduction to *The Reversible World: Symbolic Inversion in Art and Society* (Ithaca: Cornell University Press, 1978), p. 32.

45. On the incompleteness of the carnival body, see Mikhail Bakhtin, *Rabelais and His World*, trans. Helene Iswolsky (Cambridge: MIT Press, 1968; reprint, Bloomington: Indiana University Press, 1984), pp. 1–13, 25–29, 44, 52. See also Stallybrass and White, *Politics and Poetics of Transgression*, pp. 8–9.

46. See Bakhtin, *Rabelais and His World*; Henri Bergson, "Laughter," in *Comedy*, ed. Wylie Sypher (New York: Doubleday, 1956; reprint, Baltimore: Johns Hopkins University Press, 1980), pp. 61–190; Sigmund Freud, *Jokes and Their Relation to the Unconscious*, trans. James Strachey (London: Routledge and Kegan Paul, 1960); Victor Turner, "Betwixt and Between: The Liminal Period in *Rites de Passage*," in *The Forest of Symbols: Aspects of Ndembu Ritual* (Ithaca: Cornell

University Press, 1967), pp. 93–111; Rodney Needham, introduction to *Primitive Classification*, by Emile Durkheim and Marcel Mauss (London: Cohen and West, 1963), pp. vii–xlviii; Natalie Zemon Davis, "Women on Top: Symbolic Sexual Inversion and Political Disorder in Early Modern Europe," in *The Reversible World: Symbolic Inversion in Art and Society*, ed. Barbara A. Babcock (Ithaca: Cornell University Press, 1978), pp. 147–90.

In addition, Karen Sánchez-Eppler concludes her study of body politic metaphors in American literature with a discussion of the topsy-turvy doll, a toy that joined a black child with a white child in the same reversible figure. "Flipping between white missey and black pickaninny," Sánchez-Eppler explains, "the doll asserts the contiguity of these two figures; they are but opposite ends of the same domestic fate" (p. 133). Far from suggesting the potential for genuine transformation, however, the appeal of such artifacts lies, Sánchez-Eppler claims, "in their ability to mask and deny a national history of miscegenation" (p. 134). *Touching Liberty: Abolition, Feminism, and the Politics of the Body* (Berkeley: University of California Press, 1993), pp. 133–41.

47. Babcock, *The Reversible World*, p. 17.

48. For an excellent discussion of the "carnival of confusion" surrounding Topsy in *Uncle Tom's Cabin*, see Arnold Weinstein, *Nobody's Home: Speech, Self, and Place in American Fiction from Hawthorne to DeLillo* (New York: Oxford University Press, 1993), pp. 56–60.

49. Woolsey, *Hospital Days*, p. 71.

50. Alcott, "My Contraband," p. 78.

51. Ibid., p. 77. See also Showalter's discussion of this division in her introduction to *Alternative Alcott*, p. xxix.

52. Walt Whitman, *Notebooks and Unpublished Prose Manuscripts*, vol. 2, ed. Edward F. Grier (New York: New York University Press, 1984), p. 591.

53. For accounts of the visual aesthetic of "sketches" in the Civil War, see James Dougherty, *Walt Whitman and the Citizen's Eye* (Baton Rouge: Louisiana State University Press, 1993), pp. 88–90, 108–35; and M. Wynn Thomas, *The Lunar Light of Whitman's Poetry* (Cambridge: Harvard University Press, 1987), pp. 127–36.

54. Quoted in Shively, *Drum Beats*, p. 59.

55. Whitman, *Correspondence*, 1: 171.

56. The phrase is from James Jackson, Jr., quoted in John Harley Warner, *The Therapeutic Perspective: Medical Practice, Knowledge, and Identity in America, 1820–1885* (Cambridge: Harvard University Press, 1986), p. 26.

57. A native Georgian and the wife of a Confederate infantry soldier, Jackson served as a nurse in Union field hospitals at Resaca and Vining's Station, Georgia, during Sherman's Campaign for Atlanta in the summer of 1864. Alert to the complexity of her position as a Southern woman in the Union army, Jackson promotes the liminality of nursing as a political as well as a psychological response to the war. Like Whitman's convalescent, the nurse lives "on both sides of the line" in Jackson's narrative, occupying what she terms the "medium ground" of political and philosophical compromise (p. 21).

58. In "Tympan" Derrida articulates as a philosophical problem, and a specific dilemma in his own writing, the power of logocentric discourse to appropriate the terms of any critique. Philosophy can recuperate anything it can understand, transcending—or, in a key term from Hegel, "sublating"—its own margin. The capacity of the tympanum "to receive and repercuss type" (p. xxvii) suggests its appropriateness as a sign of this discourse, and what Whitman, working from a similar set of Hegelian assumptions, seems most to desire. The coincidental prominence of liminal figures like the tympan, the incest taboo, and the *pharmakon* for both Whitman and Derrida should not obscure the obvious differences between these writers. Like Derrida, Whitman exposes unrecuperable elements that cross over closed or totalitarian forms of thought. But this crossing does not presage a textual deconstruction. Indeed Whitman identifies such uncertainty with a democratic theory of representation. I point out this issue to acknowledge the way in which my own appropriation of the "tympan"— in the service of Whitman's democratic humanism—is precisely what worries Derrida's essay. See "Tympan," in *Margins of Philosophy*, trans. Alan Bass (Chicago: University of Chicago Press, 1982), pp. ix–xxix.

59. This emphasis reverses the direction of some critical commentary on Whitman. Sanctioned by the poet's appeals to Union, Whitman's readers consistently, and often persuasively, construct his Civil War writings as a closed rather than a suspended poetic narrative—a passage from individual grief to philosophical resolution (George Fredrickson), from a heterodox poetry of the body to the conventionalities of the Victorian soul (M. Jimmie Killingsworth), or from the meaninglessness of suffering to the ideology of war (Timothy Sweet). These accounts, like many others, call attention to some form of political, psychological, or ideological closure in *Drum-Taps*—a linear advance that rules out and leaves behind a prior heterogeneity (grief, meaninglessness, the body). See Fredrickson, *The Inner Civil War*, pp. 90–97; M. Jimmie Killingsworth, *Whitman's Poetry of the Body: Sexuality, Politics, and the Text* (Chapel Hill:

University of North Carolina Press, 1989), pp. 131–44; and Timothy Sweet, *Traces of War: Poetry, Photography, and the Crisis of the Union* (Baltimore: Johns Hopkins University Press, 1990), pp. 11–45. A uniform or undeviating closure is not the sign of philosophical resolution for Whitman, nor of poetic or ideological stability. It is the sign of the dead or the near dead, figures who are incapable of complex response and indifferent to medical and literary attention.

60. Derrida makes this point in "Otobiographies," an essay in which he discusses the structure of the ear as a perceiving organ and its relation both to autobiography and to interpretation. See "Otobiographies: The Teaching of Nietzsche and the Politics of the Proper Name," trans. Avital Ronell, in *The Ear of the Other: Otobiography, Transference, Translation*, ed. Christie V. McDonald (New York: Schocken Books, 1985), p. 33.

61. See Sean Wilentz, *Chants Democratic: New York City and the Rise of the American Working Class, 1788–1850* (New York: Oxford University Press, 1984), pp. 107–42.

62. Horace Traubel, ed., *With Walt Whitman in Camden*, vol. 2 (New York: Rowman and Littlefield, 1961), p. 29, quoted in Thomas, *The Lunar Light of Whitman's Poetry*, p. 177.

63. Michael Moon, *Disseminating Whitman: Revision and Corporeality in "Leaves of Grass"* (Cambridge: Harvard University Press, 1991), p. 59. Moon provides a compelling example of sexual doubleness in *Drum-Taps* in his discussion of the maternal phallus in "Song of the Banner at Daybreak" and "By Blue Ontario's Shore," pp. 175–76, 184–89, 192–93, 200–201, 206–7.

64. William Faulkner, *Absalom, Absalom!* (New York: Random House, 1972), p. 261.

65. Edgar A. Dryden, *The Form of American Romance* (Baltimore: Johns Hopkins University Press, 1988), p. 147. Throughout *Drum-Taps* Whitman imagines the expansion of self-contained figures in terms of a musical repercussion, an idea that occurs also to Hemingway in his novel of the Spanish Civil War, *For Whom the Bell Tolls*. Opening with a quotation from Donne's *Devotions*—"No man is an *Iland*, intire of it selfe"—Hemingway demonstrates the impossibility of containing the expansive effects of war. Blowing up a bridge, delaying a cavalry advance, planning an invasion—such strategic acts depend on a model of causality that proves untenable in Robert Jordan's actual experience of war. The frequent critical observation that *Drum-Taps* fails to represent specific combat—"Men suffer, die, grieve and are mourned, and they contemplate the fact of war, but no one shoots a gun," Denise T. Askin notes—identifies as a kind of moral failure a rep-

resentation of war that obscures the agency of single figures. Yet it is precisely that singularity—a battle, a death, a figure of speech "intire of it selfe"—that civil war contradicts for Whitman and Hemingway. See Denise T. Askin, "Retrievements Out of the Night: Prophetic and Private Voices in Whitman's *Drum Taps*," *American Transcendental Quarterly* 51 (summer 1981), p. 222.

66. Mark Maslan emphasizes the connections among death, writing, and absence in "Come Up from the Fields Father." For Maslan, the transformation of the body into writing depends on a prior dissociation of body and person in death. "[T]he body becomes the text," Maslan argues, "by becoming dead" (p. 945). According to Maslan, the mother realizes and responds to this dissociation as she notes the letter's "strange hand." See "Whitman's 'Strange Hand': Body as Text in *Drum-Taps*," *ELH* 58 (1991), pp. 935–55.

67. See Eric J. Sundquist, *Faulkner: The House Divided* (Baltimore: Johns Hopkins University Press, 1983), pp. 28–43.

68. See, for example, C. Carroll Hollis, *Language and Style in "Leaves of Grass"* (Baton Rouge: Louisiana State University Press, 1983), pp. 65–123.

69. Alan Trachtenberg, "Whitman's Romance of the Body: A Note on 'This Compost,'" in *Medicine and Literature*, ed. Enid Rhodes Peschel (New York: N. Watson Academic Publications, 1980), p. 192.

70. Roger Gilbert, "From Anxiety to Power: Grammar and Crisis in 'Crossing Brooklyn Ferry,'" *Nineteenth-Century Literature* 42 (December 1987), p. 341.

71. Derrida, "Tympan," p. xiv.

72. Gilbert, "From Anxiety to Power," p. 341.

73. Walt Whitman, "A Song for Occupations" (1855), in *Walt Whitman: Complete Poetry and Collected Prose*, ed. Justin Kaplan (New York: Literary Classics of the United States, 1982), p. 96.

74. I am relying here on Derrida's "Tympan" and Geoffrey Ashall Glaister, *Glaister's Glossary of the Book* (Berkeley: University of California Press, 1979).

CHAPTER THREE

1. Walt Whitman, *November Boughs*, in *Walt Whitman: Complete Poetry and Collected Prose*, ed. Justin Kaplan (New York: Literary Classics of the United States, 1982), pp. 1216–17.

2. See M. Wynn Thomas, *The Lunar Light of Whitman's Poetry* (Cambridge: Harvard University Press, 1987), pp. 178–204.

3. Walt Whitman, *Walt Whitman's "Memoranda During the War" and Death*

of Abraham Lincoln, ed. Roy P. Basler (Bloomington: Indiana University Press, 1962), p. 64.

4. On the relation between sympathy and social control in Whitman, see Thomas, *Lunar Light of Whitman's Poetry*, p. 160.

5. James M. Cox, "Walt Whitman, Mark Twain, and the Civil War," *Sewanee Review* 69, no. 2 (spring 1961), p. 191.

6. Walt Whitman, "When Lilacs Last in the Dooryard Bloom'd," in *Drum-Taps (1865) and Sequel to Drum-Taps (1865–66): A Facsimile Reproduction*, ed. F. DeWolfe Miller (Gainesville, Fla.: Scholars' Facsimiles and Reprints, 1959), p. 10.

7. Walt Whitman, *Democratic Vistas*, in *Walt Whitman: Complete Poetry and Collected Prose*, ed. Justin Kaplan (New York: Literary Classics of the United States, 1982), p. 961. Joseph Cady explores a similar tension between Whitman's Emersonian faith in correspondence and a gay sensibility at odds with the assumptions of a popular audience. See "Not Happy in the Capitol: Homosexuality and the Calamus Poems," *American Studies* 19, no. 2 (fall 1978), p. 7.

8. See Ezra Greenspan, *Walt Whitman and the American Reader* (Cambridge: Cambridge University Press, 1990), p. 96.

9. Walt Whitman, Preface (1855), in *Walt Whitman: Complete Poetry and Collected Prose*, ed. Justin Kaplan (New York: Literary Classics of the United States, 1982), p. 26.

10. Walt Whitman, *Walt Whitman: The Correspondence*, vol. 1, ed. Edwin Haviland Miller (New York: New York University Press, 1961), p. 52.

11. See George B. Forgie, *Patricide in the House Divided: A Psychological Interpretation of Lincoln and His Age* (New York: W. W. Norton, 1979), pp. 4, 159–99.

12. Jane Tompkins, *Sensational Designs: The Cultural Work of American Fiction, 1790–1860* (New York: Oxford University Press, 1985), pp. 150–51.

13. Whitman, *Memoranda During the War*, p. 5. See also Walt Whitman, *Specimen Days*, in *Walt Whitman: Complete Poetry and Collected Prose*, ed. Justin Kaplan (New York: Literary Classics of the United States, 1982), p. 779. Subsequent quotations from *Specimen Days* in this chapter will be cited in the text by page number.

14. George Hutchinson stresses this transference in *The Ecstatic Whitman: Literary Shamanism and the Crisis of the Union* (Columbus: Ohio State University Press, 1986), p. 2.

15. Walt Whitman, *Notebooks and Unpublished Prose Manuscripts*, vol. 2, ed. Edward F. Grier (New York: New York University Press, 1984), p. 567.

16. Philip Fisher, *Hard Facts: Setting and Form in the American Novel* (New York: Oxford University Press, 1987), pp. 118–19.

17. Walt Whitman, *Prose Works, 1892*, vol. 1, ed. Floyd Stovall (New York: New York University Press, 1963), p. 302.

18. Harriet Beecher Stowe, *Uncle Tom's Cabin*, ed. Ann Douglas (New York: Penguin Books, 1981), p. 144.

19. Ibid., p. 149.

20. Ibid., p. 154.

21. Ibid.

22. Louisa May Alcott, *Hospital Sketches*, in *Alternative Alcott*, ed. Elaine Showalter (New Brunswick, N.J.: Rutgers University Press, 1988), p. 22.

23. See Fisher, *Hard Facts*, pp. 99–104.

24. *The Wound Dresser*, in *The Complete Writings of Walt Whitman*, vol. 4, ed. Richard Maurice Bucke (New York: G. P. Putnam's Sons, 1902), p. 100.

25. Whitman, *Correspondence*, 1: 205.

26. Katharine Prescott Wormeley, *The Other Side of War with the Army of the Potomac* (Boston: Ticknor, 1889), p. 145.

27. Whitman, *Prose Works, 1892*, 1: 302.

28. Whitman, *Drum-Taps*, p. 40.

29. Ibid.

30. Whitman, *November Boughs*, p. 1217.

31. Mark Maslan discusses the thematic and narrative links between "Come Up from the Fields Father" and "Vigil Strange" in "Whitman's 'Strange Hand': Body as Text in *Drum-Taps*," *ELH* 58 (1991), pp. 943–44.

32. Whitman, *Drum-Taps*, p. 42.

33. Kerry C. Larson makes this point in *Whitman's Drama of Consensus* (Chicago: University of Chicago Press, 1988), pp. 207–44.

34. Whitman, *Drum-Taps*, p. 43.

35. Ibid., p. 49.

36. Whitman, *Correspondence*, 1: 111.

37. Ibid., p. 77.

38. Whitman, Preface (1855), p. 26.

39. Whitman, *Drum-Taps*, pp. 31–33.

40. Whitman, *The Wound Dresser*, 4: 119.

41. Drawing on White, as well as Toril Moi and Julia Kristeva, M. Jimmie Killingsworth provides an excellent account of the sexual and political implications of Whitman's tropes. See *Whitman's Poetry of the Body: Sexuality, Politics, and the Text* (Chapel Hill: University of North Carolina Press, 1989), p. xiv.

42. This formulation is indebted to Mitchell Robert Breitwieser's discussion of grief and typology in *American Puritanism and the Defense of Mourning: Religion, Grief, and Ethnology in Mary White Rowlandson's Captivity Narrative* (Madison: University of Wisconsin Press, 1990), pp. 3–70.

43. On this quality in Hawthorne, see Gordon Hutner, *Secrets and Sympathy: Forms of Disclosure in Hawthorne's Novels* (Athens: University of Georgia Press, 1988), pp. 12–13.

44. Whitman, *Memoranda During the War*, pp. 27–28.

45. Henry D. Thoreau, *Walden*, ed. J. Lyndon Shanley (Princeton: Princeton University Press, 1971), p. 318.

CHAPTER FOUR

1. Walt Whitman, *Notebooks and Unpublished Prose Manuscripts*, vol. 2, ed. Edward F. Grier (New York: New York University Press, 1984), pp. 575, 659.

2. Walter Lowenfels, ed., *Walt Whitman's Civil War* (New York: Alfred A. Knopf, 1961; reprint, New York: Da Capo Press, 1989), p. 12.

3. Walt Whitman, *Walt Whitman's "Memoranda During the War" and Death of Abraham Lincoln*, ed. Roy P. Basler (Bloomington: Indiana University Press, 1962), p. 5. Subsequent quotations from the *Memoranda* in this chapter will be cited in the text by page number.

4. Walt Whitman, *Democratic Vistas*, in *Walt Whitman: Complete Poetry and Collected Prose*, ed. Justin Kaplan (New York: Literary Classics of the United States, 1982), p. 989. On the importance of free labor to Whitman's understanding of the Civil War, see M. Wynn Thomas, *The Lunar Light of Whitman's Poetry* (Cambridge: Harvard University Press, 1987), pp. 178–204.

5. Daniel Aaron, *The Unwritten War: American Writers and the Civil War* (New York: Alfred A. Knopf, 1973; reprint, Madison: University of Wisconsin Press, 1987), p. 338.

6. John De Forest, "Caesar's Art of War and of Writing," *The Atlantic Monthly* 44 (September 1879), pp. 287–88.

7. Wolcott Gibbs, quoted in Aaron, *The Unwritten War*, p. 150.

8. Aaron, *The Unwritten War*, pp. 34–38.

9. Walt Whitman, *Leaves of Grass (1891–92)*, in *Walt Whitman: Complete Poetry and Collected Prose*, ed. Justin Kaplan (New York: Literary Classics of the United States, 1982), pp. 465–66.

10. Walt Whitman, *Specimen Days*, in *Walt Whitman: Complete Poetry and Collected Prose*, ed. Justin Kaplan (New York: Literary Classics of the United States, 1982), p. 778.

11. De Forest, "Caesar's Art of War and of Writing," p. 286.

12. Walt Whitman, *A Backward Glance o'er Travel'd Roads*, in *Walt Whitman: Complete Poetry and Collected Prose*, ed. Justin Kaplan (New York: Literary Classics of the United States, 1982), p. 657.

13. Betsy Erkkila stresses this issue in her reading of the *Memoranda*: "The main substance of Whitman's *Memoranda* is not the issues that provoked the war but, rather, the character displayed by the American people during the war." *Whitman the Political Poet* (New York: Oxford University Press, 1989), p. 208.

14. Ralph Waldo Emerson, "Character," in *Essays and Lectures*, ed. Joel Porte (New York: Literary Classics of the United States, 1983), p. 495.

15. Jerome Loving, *Emerson, Whitman, and the American Muse* (Chapel Hill: University of North Carolina Press, 1982), pp. 55–82.

16. Whitman, *Leaves of Grass*, p. 269.

17. Ibid., p. 270.

18. Michael T. Gilmore describes a similar effect in Ishmael's narrative stance in *Moby-Dick*. See *American Romanticism and the Marketplace* (Chicago: University of Chicago Press, 1985), p. 120.

19. Whitman, *Leaves of Grass*, p. 283; *Notebooks*, 2: 669.

20. Richard H. Shryock, "A Medical Perspective on the Civil War," *American Quarterly* 14, no. 2 (summer 1962), p. 167.

21. Louisa May Alcott, *Hospital Sketches*, in *Alternative Alcott*, ed. Elaine Showalter (New Brunswick, N.J.: Rutgers University Press, 1988), p. 70. See also Whitman's remark to Traubel about medical care: "they doctor a man as a disease not as a man: a part of him—doctor a part of him: a leg, a belly, an eye: they ignore the rest." Horace Traubel, ed., *With Walt Whitman in Camden*, vol. 3 (New York: M. Kennerley, 1914), p. 294, quoted in Harold Aspiz, *Walt Whitman and the Body Beautiful* (Urbana: University of Illinois Press, 1980), p. 104.

22. Michel Foucault, *The Birth of the Clinic: An Archeology of Medical Perception*, trans. A. M. Sheridan Smith (New York: Vintage Books, 1975), p. 166.

23. Ibid., pp. 59, 146, 166, 196.

24. Ibid., p. 95.

25. John Rawls, *A Theory of Justice* (Cambridge: The Belknap Press of Harvard University Press, 1971), p. 137, quoted in Martha Banta, "Medical Therapies and the Body Politic," *Prospects* 8 (1983), p. 114.

26. See George M. Fredrickson, *The Inner Civil War: Northern Intellectuals and the Crisis of the Union* (New York: Harper and Row, 1965), p. 89.

27. Friedrich Nietzsche, *The Gay Science*, trans. Walter Kaufmann (New York: Vintage Books, 1974), p. 38. For a very different analysis of Whitman's visual aesthetic, see James Dougherty, *Walt Whitman and the Citizen's Eye* (Baton Rouge: Louisiana State University Press, 1993), pp. 76–139. Dougherty puts a new spin on the old story of Whitman's political and creative decline after the Civil War. Where others read that decline in terms of the poet's conflicted sexuality (Stephen Black, M. Jimmie Killingsworth) or his weakening belief in the "word magic" of performative utterance (C. Carroll Hollis, Tenney Nathanson) or his despair in the possibility of radical democracy (Kerry C. Larson, M. Wynn Thomas), Dougherty sees that decline in visual terms. He argues that Whitman created an economy of images in his Civil War writings well suited to the popular tastes of a mass audience. Turning to a conventionalized pictorial aesthetic, Whitman choked down a skepticism Dougherty associates with the Satan of "Chanting the Square Deific" and rose from the ashes of war transformed into the good gray poet. Whitman's sexuality, his voice, and now even his eyes are reshaped to a middle-class standard. Needless to say, I find Whitman's visual aesthetic in the Civil War more original and revisionary, particularly as it takes shape in his hospital narrative. Dougherty pays little attention to that narrative, except to misname and misdate it as "*War Memoranda* (1873)" (p. 88).

28. In a notebook entry in 1856 Whitman had set a very different task for himself as a writer: "A poem in which is minutely described the whole particulars and ensemble of a *first-rate healthy Human Body*—it looks into and through, as if it were transparent and of fine glass." Quoted in Aspiz, *Walt Whitman and the Body Beautiful*, p. 68. Whitman's formulation here is similar to the "unobstructed transparency" of Foucault's clinic. Aspiz connects this transparency to Whitman's interest in anatomy charts and pathognomy, representations that open the body to a penetrating gaze. It is exactly that gaze that Whitman obstructs in his hospital writings, occluding the corporeal transparency he once

sought to achieve. But that change is motivated by a specifically political response to power—not by sublimation, timidity, or homosexual guilt.

29. Foucault, *The Birth of the Clinic*, p. 166.

30. Such scenes complicate characterizations of Whitman's language as "primal" or "unmediated." Allen Grossman, for instance, stresses the "primal communication" of Whitman's speech—an inarticulate "hum" open to sexual and political union. Unselective and diffuse, Whitman's language resists "the mechanical checks and balances" of political constitutionalism. Grossman claims that by releasing language from obstruction—"hermeneutic bondage"—the poet restores consciousness to a state undeformed by mediation. This claim is elaborated by Donald E. Pease, who argues that the subvocal hum of poetic voice connotes the recovery of political consensus—a self-evident consensus that "goes without saying." See Allen Grossman, "The Poetics of Union in Whitman and Lincoln: An Inquiry toward the Relationship of Art and Policy," in *The American Renaissance Reconsidered: Selected Papers from the English Institute, 1982–83*, ed. Walter Benn Michaels and Donald E. Pease (Baltimore: Johns Hopkins University Press, 1985), pp. 195, 194, 200; and Donald E. Pease, *Visionary Compacts: American Renaissance Writings in Cultural Contexts* (Madison: University of Wisconsin Press, 1987), p. 144. What goes without saying is the revision of this idea in the Washington hospitals. The primal and the unmediated become profoundly unattractive when one is hurt. And Whitman seeks to make prominent rather than to disguise the checks and balances of his text.

31. Foucault, *The Birth of the Clinic*, pp. 95, 196.

32. Ludmilla Jordanova, *Sexual Visions: Images of Gender in Science and Medicine between the Eighteenth and Twentieth Centuries* (Madison: University of Wisconsin Press, 1989), p. 158.

33. Roger Asselineau, *The Evolution of Walt Whitman: The Creation of a Personality* (Cambridge: Harvard University Press, 1960), p. 172.

34. Ibid., p. 71.

35. Sublimation is the key issue in treatments of Whitman's hospital experience by Daniel Aaron ("he sublimated and legitimized his homosexual impulses"), and Justin Kaplan ("a delicate structure of denial and sublimation"). Read as sanctioned deflections of an illicit erotic, Whitman's hospital work gains, in these accounts, something of what F. O. Matthiessen once called the "vaguely pathological" quality of Whitman's homosexuality, a quality that Paul

Zweig emphasizes in his discussion of Whitman's nursing: "Whitman's self, bathed in the erotic, fed on suffering; it lived off the helplessness of a dying generation. No wonder then that these 'contradictions' tore him apart and finally helped to make him sick." See Aaron, *The Unwritten War*, p. 65; Justin Kaplan, *Walt Whitman: A Life* (New York: Simon and Schuster, 1980), p. 296; F. O. Matthiessen, *American Renaissance: Art and Expression in the Age of Emerson and Whitman* (London: Oxford University Press, 1941), p. 535; and Paul Zweig, *Walt Whitman: The Making of the Poet* (New York: Basic Books, 1984), p. 343. In disputing accounts of sublimation, Joseph Cady articulates a view closer to my own. See "*Drum-Taps* and Nineteenth-Century Male Homosexual Literature," in *Walt Whitman: Here and Now*, ed. Joann P. Krieg (Westport, Conn.: Greenwood Press, 1985), pp. 49–59.

36. Quoted in Edward Carpenter, *Days with Walt Whitman* (London: Allen, 1906), p. 43.

37. Timothy Sweet, *Traces of War: Poetry, Photography, and the Crisis of the Union* (Baltimore: Johns Hopkins University Press, 1990), pp. 46–77.

38. Ibid., p. 77.

39. Ibid., p. 51.

40. The consummate realism of Thomas Eakins's *Gross Clinic*, for example, identifies as masculine the ability to see directly. The *Gross Clinic* represents the triumph of masculine realism (and its attendant values of clarity and proportion) over the oblique, literally foreshortened, figure of the woman. For many American writers this image is a condensed summary of the meaning of the Civil War: the feminine (the Southern, the romantic) is displaced and marginalized by the pragmatism, instrumentality, and masculine authority of the Union army. Samuel Gross—a Union officer and author of a manual of military surgery—personifies those values. He towers over the turned in and helpless figure of the woman, who forms the literal and ideological background for a realistic perception of the wound. The woman is made to display as a legitimating sign of masculine authority the very difference produced by that authority in the first place. A woman in 1875 could not, with rare exceptions, perform surgery. Quite literally, she could not—unlike Eakins and Gross—see directly. The woman is defeated artistically by the representational values of Eakins's image, just as she is defeated in fact by the exclusionary social values the image legitimates. In the classic operation of ideology, she is made to produce the signs of her own subjection. On this, see Michael Fried, "Realism, Writing, and Disfiguration in

Thomas Eakins's *Gross Clinic*, with a Postscript on Stephen Crane's Upturned Faces," *Representations* 9 (winter 1985), pp. 33–104.

41. For a discussion of how medical discourse in Poe permits the horror of mutilation, see Mary Catherine Cappello, *Writing the Spirit/Reading the Mind: Representations of Illness and Health in Nineteenth-Century American Literature* (Ann Arbor, Mich.: University Microfilms International, 1990), pp. 157–58.

42. Anonymous, *Notes of Hospital Life* (Philadelphia: Lippincott, 1864), p. 168.

43. Walt Whitman, *Prose Works 1892*, vol. 1, ed. Floyd Stovall (New York: New York University Press, 1963), p. 297.

44. Whitman, *Democratic Vistas*, p. 956.

45. For Whitman's adaptation of the epic tradition, see James E. Miller, Jr., *The American Quest for a Supreme Fiction: Whitman's Legacy in the Personal Epic* (Chicago: University of Chicago Press, 1979), pp. 30–49; and *"Leaves of Grass": America's Lyric-Epic of Self and Democracy* (New York: Twayne, 1992), pp. 23–35.

46. Kenneth Burke, "Towards Looking Back," *Journal of General Education* 28 (fall 1976), pp. 185–86. See also Betsy Erkkila's discussion of this issue in *Whitman the Political Poet*, pp. 140–54.

47. Walt Whitman, *Drum-Taps*, p. 47.

48. These phrases are from Whitman's depiction of heterosexual love in "Fast-Anchor'd Eternal O Love!" *Leaves of Grass (1891–92)*, p. 285.

49. Whitman, *Drum-Taps*, p. 48.

50. Ibid., pp. 48–49.

51. Tenney Nathanson stresses this dimension of Whitman's art in *Whitman's Presence: Body, Voice, and Writing in "Leaves of Grass"* (New York: New York University Press, 1992). Nathanson shows how Whitman sought to express an experience of living plenitude through the "word magic" of the great early poems. Overcoming the division between subject and object, Whitman chants into being an "archaic" world of pure presence. In such a world, the poet enjoys an expressive relation untouched by the entanglements and obstructions of writing, the poisoned apple in this fable. Representation marks the loss of that archaic world, a fall into difference and division, a lapse into writing and textuality. Like Allen Grossman and Donald E. Pease, Nathanson sees Whitman's goal as nothing less than "the banishing of representation" (p. 78), "the liberation from representation and its defects" (p. 76).

Can a democratic poet "banish" representation? Can he avoid immersion in political and symbolic processes that are inevitably imperfect and incomplete? As George Hutchinson has noted, Nathanson offers little help in understanding the relationship between the magical transformations of the first two editions of *Leaves of Grass* and the democratic ambitions Whitman set for himself throughout his career. Indeed Nathanson dismisses those ambitions as "melodramatic" and "maudlin"—"awkward efforts to displace to the domain of public policy visions of danger and possibility that originate elsewhere" (p. 21). Such a view prevents Nathanson from seeing much value in Whitman's career after 1860, a period in which the poet explored with great force the meaning of democratic representation. Nathanson's notion of a "fall from completeness" (p. 94) provides, I believe, a powerful way of marking this change in Whitman's career. But I see that change not as a sign of Whitman's declining powers as a shaman-poet, as Nathanson does, but as a sign of his increasing powers as a democratic poet, a poet for whom knowledge is necessarily and desirably incomplete. See George Hutchinson, review of *Whitman's Presence: Body, Voice, and Writing in "Leaves of Grass,"* by Tenney Nathanson, *Modern Philology* 92 (May 1995), pp. 520–23.

52. "The Oven Bird," in *The Poetry of Robert Frost*, ed. Edward Connery Lathem (New York: Henry Holt, 1969), p. 120.

53. On the "grand conception" of the 1855 and 1856 *Leaves of Grass*, see Zweig, *Walt Whitman: The Making of the Poet*, pp. 276–79.

54. Robert Penn Warren, *The Legacy of the Civil War: Meditations on the Centennial* (New York: Random House, 1961), p. 22. Wolcott Gibbs, quoted in Aaron, *The Unwritten War*, p. 150.

55. Walt Whitman, *Walt Whitman: The Correspondence*, vol. 3, ed. Edwin Haviland Miller (New York: New York University Press, 1964), p. 382. William Aarnes calls attention to the significance of this phrase in "'Cut This Out': Whitman Liberating the Reader in *Specimen Days,*" *Walt Whitman Review* 27 (March 1981), pp. 30–31. For a similar argument regarding Thoreau's late work, see Mitchell Robert Breitwieser, "Thoreau and the Wrecks on *Cape Cod,*" *Studies in Romanticism* 20 (spring 1981), pp. 3–20.

56. Whitman chose this title for an 1882 collection of prose fragments. See *Complete Poetry and Collected Prose*, ed. Justin Kaplan (New York: Literary Classics of the United States, 1982), pp. 1050–75.

57. Ibid., p. 1050.

58. Foucault, *Birth of the Clinic*, p. 196.

59. Jacques Derrida, *Dissemination*, trans. Barbara Johnson (Chicago: University of Chicago Press, 1981), p. 8.

60. As Whitman explores this issue in the *Memoranda*, he anticipates a larger conflict taking shape in his late work. Whitman's literary remains—what he calls "the pieces of Prose and Poetry left over"—bear the same relation to his official text the remains of the war bear to his official America. As Whitman consolidates his writing after the war he calls attention to an irreducible excess, a sense of "left-overness," compromising his own comprehensive ambitions. The key words in the titles of Whitman's late prose—"items," "cases," "laggards," "rejoinders," "splinters," "jottings," "notes at random," "notes (such as they are)," "notes left over"—unsettle comprehensive authority and provide a social and literary force of *restance*.

61. Whitman, *Specimen Days*, pp. 780–81.

62. Walt Whitman, *November Boughs*, in *Walt Whitman: Complete Poetry and Collected Prose*, ed. Justin Kaplan (New York: Literary Classics of the United States, 1982), p. 1137.

63. Alcott, *Hospital Sketches*, p. 58.

64. Nathaniel Hawthorne, *The Marble Faun* (New York: New American Library, 1961), p. 37.

65. Whitman, *Correspondence*, 3: 315.

CHAPTER FIVE

1. Richard Selzer, "Pages from a Wound-Dresser's Diary," in *Confessions of a Knife* (New York: Simon and Schuster, 1979; reprint, New York: William Morrow, 1987), pp. 133–48.

2. Richard Selzer, Preface (1987), *Mortal Lessons: Notes on the Art of Surgery* (New York: Simon and Schuster, 1974; reprint, Touchstone, 1987), p. 7.

3. Ralph Waldo Emerson, "Intellect," in *Essays and Lectures*, ed. Joel Porte (New York: Literary Classics of the United States, 1983), p. 426.

4. On the cultural obsolescence of Whitman's Civil War writings, see M. Wynn Thomas, *The Lunar Light of Whitman's Poetry* (Cambridge: Harvard University Press, 1987), p. 2. I also note that in a recent reassessment of Whitman's career none of the articles tracing Whitman's influence mention the poet's hospital writings or consider his influence in the field of literature and medicine. See "The Influence: Whitman among Others," in *Walt Whitman. The Centennial*

Essays, ed. Ed Folsom (Iowa City: University of Iowa Press, 1994), pp. 184–250. This section includes essays by James E. Miller Jr., George B. Hutchinson, Kenneth M. Price, Walter Grünzweig, and V. K. Chari.

5. Walt Whitman, *Walt Whitman's "Memoranda During the War" and Death of Abraham Lincoln*, ed. Roy P. Basler (Bloomington: Indiana University Press, 1962), p. 65.

6. Quoted in Charles I. Schuster, "The Nonfictional Prose of Richard Selzer: An Aesthetic Analysis," in *Literary Nonfiction: Theory, Criticism, Pedagogy*, ed. Chris Anderson (Carbondale: Southern Illinois University Press, 1989), p. 20.

7. Selzer, "Pages from a Wound-Dresser's Diary," p. 134.

8. Ibid., pp. 140–41.

9. Ibid., p. 135.

10. Walt Whitman, *Walt Whitman: The Correspondence*, vol. 1, ed. Edwin Haviland Miller (New York: New York University Press, 1961), p. 93.

11. Selzer, "Pages from a Wound-Dresser's Diary," p. 141.

12. Ibid., p. 143.

13. Walt Whitman, "Crossing Brooklyn Ferry," in *Walt Whitman: Complete Poetry and Collected Prose*, ed. Justin Kaplan (New York: Literary Classics of the United States, 1982), p. 309.

14. Selzer, "Pages from a Wound-Dresser's Diary," p. 138.

15. Ibid., pp. 147–48.

16. Richard Selzer, "The Pen and the Scalpel," *New York Times Magazine*, August 21, 1988, p. 31.

17. Barbara Herrnstein Smith, *Poetic Closure: A Study of How Poems End* (Chicago: University of Chicago Press, 1968), p. 36. For a summary of theories of closure, see Wallace Martin, *Recent Theories of Narrative* (Ithaca: Cornell University Press, 1986), pp. 83–90; and Elizabeth J. MacArthur, *Extravagant Narratives: Closure and Dynamics in the Epistolary Form* (Princeton: Princeton University Press, 1990), pp. 3–35. For a study of closure in American short fiction, see John Gerlach, *Toward the End: Closure and Structure in the American Short Story* (University, Ala.: The University of Alabama Press, 1985).

18. Howard Brody, *Stories of Sickness* (New Haven: Yale University Press, 1987), pp. 9 n. 4 and 30. In this formulation Brody is drawing on Arthur Kleinman, Leon Eisenberg, and Byron Good, "Culture, Illness, and Care: Clinical Lessons from Anthropologic and Cross-Cultural Research," *Annals of Internal Medicine* 88 (February 1978), pp. 251–58; and Frank Kermode, *The Sense of an*

Ending: Studies in the Theory of Fiction (New York: Oxford University Press, 1967).

19. Richard Selzer, "Imelda," in *Letters to a Young Doctor* (New York: Simon and Schuster, 1982), p. 27.

20. Victor Kestenbaum, "Introduction: The Experience of Illness," in *The Humanity of the Ill: Phenomenological Perspectives*, ed. Victor Kestenbaum (Knoxville: University of Tennessee Press, 1982), p. 18. Kestenbaum derives this imperative—"to restore the patient's humanity"—from Edmund D. Pellegrino, *Humanism and the Physician* (Knoxville: University of Tennessee Press, 1979), p. 123.

21. Richard Selzer, "Brute," in *Letters to a Young Doctor* (New York: Simon and Schuster, 1982), p. 61.

22. Ibid., p. 62.

23. See Jacques-Alain Miller, "Suture," *Screen* 18 (winter 1977–78), pp. 24–34; Jean-Pierre Oudart, "Cinema and Suture," *Screen* 18 (winter 1977–78), pp. 35–47; Daniel Dayan, "The Tutor-Code of Classical Cinema," in *Movies and Methods: An Anthology*, ed. Bill Nichols (Berkeley: University of California Press, 1976), pp. 438–51; Stephen Heath, "On Suture," in *Questions of Cinema* (Bloomington: Indiana University Press, 1981), pp. 76–112; and Kaja Silverman, "Suture," in *The Subject of Semiotics* (New York: Oxford University Press, 1983), pp. 194–236. For an analysis of the relation between suture theory and Lacanian psychoanalysis, see Heath, "On Suture," pp. 76–86. For a cogent critique of suture theory, see Noël Carroll, "Address to the Heathen," *October* 23 (winter 1981), pp. 89–163. Wolfgang Kemp draws on reader-response theory in his use of the suture as a concept in historical painting; see "Death at Work: A Case Study on Constitutive Blanks in Nineteenth-Century Painting," *Representations* 10 (spring 1985), pp. 102–23. I have also profited from Susan Schweik's discussion of suture in "A Needle with Mama's Voice: Mitsuye Yamada's *Camp Notes* and the American Canon of War Poetry," in *Arms and the Woman: War, Gender, and Literary Representation*, ed. Helen M. Cooper, Adrienne Auslander Munich, and Susan Merrill Squier (Chapel Hill: University of North Carolina Press, 1989), pp. 225–43. No one to my knowledge has applied the concept of the suture to medical and surgical narrative.

24. Silverman, "Suture," pp. 206, 213.

25. Ibid., p. 212.

26. Ibid., pp. 231–32.

27. Ibid., p. 205.

28. Dayan, "The Tutor-Code of Classical Cinema," p. 449.

29. Carroll, "Address to the Heathen," p. 127.

30. See, for example, Jane Gallop's account of the therapeutic goal of Lacanian psychoanalysis: "Lacan's major statement of ethical purpose and therapeutic goal, as far as I am concerned, is that one must assume one's castration. . . . Lacan's message that everyone, regardless of his or her organs, is 'castrated,' represents not a loss but a gain. Only this realization, I believe, can release us from 'phallocentrism,' one of the effects of which is that one must constantly cover one's inevitable inadequacy in order to have the right to speak." *Reading Lacan* (Ithaca: Cornell University Press, 1985), p. 20.

31. Brody, *Stories of Sickness*, p. 5.

32. Selzer, "The Knife," in *Mortal Lessons: Notes on the Art of Surgery* (New York: Simon and Schuster, 1974; reprint, Touchstone, 1987), p. 101.

33. On the contrastive or "dialogic" nature of Selzer's narratives, see Charles I. Schuster, "The Nonfictional Prose of Richard Selzer," pp. 3–28. On the concept of "the open-ended present," see M. M. Bakhtin, "Epic and Novel," in *The Dialogic Imagination: Four Essays*, ed. Michael Holquist, trans. Caryl Emerson and Michael Holquist (Austin: University of Texas Press, 1981), pp. 3–40.

34. Richard Selzer, "Alexis St. Martin," in *Confessions of a Knife* (New York: Simon and Schuster, 1979; reprint, New York: William Morrow, 1987), p. 120.

35. Ibid., pp. 127–28.

36. Ibid., pp. 128, 124–25.

37. Ibid., p. 126.

38. Richard Selzer, "Letter to a Young Surgeon—II," in *Letters to a Young Doctor* (New York: Simon and Schuster, 1982), p. 52.

39. Selzer, "Imelda," p. 28.

40. Ibid., p. 27.

41. Ibid., pp. 28–29.

42. Selzer, "Sarcophagus," in *Confessions of a Knife*, p. 54.

43. Ibid., p. 55.

44. Selzer, "Amazons," in *Confessions of a Knife*, p. 39.

45. Bakhtin, *The Dialogic Imagination*, p. 32.

46. Jonathan Culler, *Flaubert: The Uses of Uncertainty* (Ithaca: Cornell University Press, 1974), p. 24.

47. D. A. Miller, *Narrative and Its Discontents: Problems of Closure in the Traditional Novel* (Princeton: Princeton University Press, 1981), p. x.

48. Selzer, "Imelda," pp. 33, 32.

49. Selzer, "Raccoon," in *Confessions of a Knife*, p. 32.

50. Ibid., p. 33.

51. Ibid., p. 34.

52. Eric J. Cassell, *The Healer's Art: A New Approach to the Doctor-Patient Relationship* (Philadelphia: Lippincott, 1976), p. 35, quoted in Charles M. Anderson, *Richard Selzer and the Rhetoric of Surgery* (Carbondale: Southern Illinois University Press, 1989), pp. 17–18.

53. Selzer, "Feet," in *Letters to a Young Doctor*, p. 174.

54. Walt Whitman, *Notebooks and Unpublished Prose Manuscripts*, vol. 2, ed. Edward F. Grier (New York: New York University Press, 1984), p. 669.

INDEX

Compositor: Braun-Brumfield, Inc.
Text: 10/15 Janson
Display: Janson
Printer and binder: Braun-Brumfield, Inc.